George Wombwell
(1777 – 1850)
Celebrated Menagerist

Volume I: Events at Warwick

By

Shaun Villiers Everett

Published by George Wombwell Collection
Social History Series

First Published in Great Britain in 2016 by George Wombwell
Collection

Copyright Shaun Villiers Everett 2016

ISBN 978-1-5262-0467-7

Address for George Wombwell Collection is
information@georgewombwell.com

THE LATE MR. WOMBWELL.

From a Pen and Ink Sketch on paper, unsigned, 1851

George Wombwell Collection (c) 2015

iv

Dedicated to my late mother,
Ruby Joyce Wombwell Everett (1918 – 2009)

Contents

1

Introduction to Series

I was asked three years ago, since I was so interested in the life of George Wombwell, if I was going to write his biography. I immediately answered 'no, there's not enough material covering his life to warrant such an adventure. Anyone going down that route is likely to expect many dead ends and will probably wish they had never started'. So, why after this time have I decided to do the very thing I warned others not to tackle? The simple answer is progress, progress with computerisation of newspaper records and the growing access to digital records around the country's many archives. These have allowed quick access to the records and as new records appeared they opened up valuable avenues of research which has led to this biography of George Wombwell to be undertaken.

I am grateful to the many contributors via the GeorgeWombwell.com website that have uncovered genealogical records and information from their own family's historical records that has guided me in certain directions or has confirmed my opinions during my own research.

This biography documents the life of the celebrated menagerist George Wombwell (1777- 1850). It is divided into three parts. *Volume One: Events at Warwick* covers a period that includes an extensively reported lion and dog fight at the Warwick racecourse during the summer of 1825. The intention of this volume is to set out the events leading up to that fight, and its immediate consequences. This notorious fight has tended to be the basis on which a characterisation of George Wombwell was fermented and one that maintains currency today in many texts, web based articles, etc. Everyone, it seems, likes the idea of the spectacle. *Events at Warwick* is very much a standalone story and although unusual in biographical publications, it warranted an edition all of its own.

Volume Two: covers the period from about 1805 to his death in

1850. Wombwell's progress to becoming the country's most celebrated Menagerist will be examined. It follows Wombwell throughout his travelling career and as a wild beast ambassador to the country at both national and international events and at Royal performances. Several newly uncovered representations will be examined to show the workings of the menagerie as it travelled around the country and how it was utilised as a site for education, exhibition and entertainment.

Volume Three: covers the period after his death to the eventual decline of the *Bostock and Wombwell* travelling menagerie during 1930s Britain. In extending this book beyond Wombwell's death, it is as much a story of the life cycle of the travelling menagerie in Britain as it is about Wombwell himself. It became obvious to me as research progressed, that Wombwell's name is synonymous with the complete story of the travelling menagerie, both here in the UK, on the continents of Europe, the USA, and on the continents of the southern hemisphere.

George Wombwell's life is also a story of modern life as seen through the eyes of travelling showmen, their families, employees and performers. Stories of their successes and also their failures and heartbreaks play a great part in determining the social history of the period. His successors and in particular, with the Bostock family association, how they maintained the same entrepreneurial spirit as Wombwell had shown half a century earlier. Wherever Wombwell travelled, he was known by the local population and was revered for his wondrous menagerie of exotic and wild beasts.

However, the name George Wombwell is probably one of 'least' best known celebrities to have travelled this island and beyond. Revered in his time across all classes, this 'celebrity' status has been much forgotten in our time. I wish to correct that view through the publication of this biography. As a travelling showman, George seems not to have put down many roots anywhere for very long. That is the nature of showmanship. However, what surprised me most was that I discovered he did have some roots at the very heart of London's fashionable society, a subject I will return to in Volume II.

So why did George Wombwell become forgotten by the public? The reasons for this are quite simple in my view. The activist's sensitivity to circuses and menageries, and in particular the mistreatment of performing animal acts, over time, has been conflated with the original work that Wombwell achieved in his efforts to introduce the natural world to a broad spectrum of the British population. The only realistic way a working class Victorian boy or girl from any provincial town across the country would see this natural world, was via the visiting menagerie or circus. What correctly followed was a deep concern for animal welfare through the introduction of progressive legislation, and travelling menageries and circuses were one of the main points of contact for twentieth century reformers. Concern for the care of wild beasts converged with the same concern for the domesticated animal and as such, animal rights became extended to circuses and menageries as they do today for zoos and safari parks. During this process, the earliest menageries such as Wombwell's, were written off as an aspect of colonial Britain, best forgotten due to their perceived cruelty, at best, and as part of the 'other' in the broader context of post-colonial discourse[1].

In Wombwell's era, what constituted animal welfare was linked to having fit and lively animals to show with good lifespans. Animals cost money and the better they are looked after, the longer they would be available for exhibition. What constitutes animal welfare today is something quite different and, in the case of circuses, involves the complete abolition of performing animals. There has been a tendency to conflate the two ends of the spectrum of past and present, thus Wombwell gets linked in with today's standards. Hence it has become fashionably pragmatic to forget the real past. Having read countless reports on Wombwell, I can think of no gentler man than the one often portrayed.

Wombwell's life seems to me very much like the life of Caravaggio, the seventeenth century artist in Rome. Involved in murderous plots and swashbuckling swordfights, Caravaggio was very much forgotten until well researched biographies appeared during the late twentieth century. Paintings remained in collections, but were often reduced to the storeroom or were put into attics to collect decades of dust and grime. Caravaggio was transformed almost overnight by these progressive biographies, to the status of a perceived artistic genius. Conversely, George Wombwell was well celebrated in his own time, but is quite forgotten today. Maybe the experiences of dealing with Caravaggio will rub off on our perception of George Wombwell.

Finally, you will find that the biography has been written using scholarly referenced material and these have been recorded as endnotes for your information, together with a complete

bibliography. If I have plagiarized any person's work, I

apologise in advance, it was certainly not intentional and credit

will be given in future editions. My excuse will always be age

and memory. What was foremost in my mind, was that this book

should be 'a good read' and I trust you find it not lacking in this

respect.

Introduction to Volume One

In the introduction I referred to the late twentieth century biographies of Caravaggio, the painter from early seventeenth century Rome. Until those biographies appeared, Caravaggio was not widely considered as a prominent court painter and the scholarship was quite small compared with the volumes of text that poured out of publishing houses on Leonardo, Michelangelo and Raphael. Although now considered a remarkable artist, in his lifetime, Caravaggio was considered the equivalent of today's standards, a 'C list' celebrity. One of the few contemporary documents that still exists today, has Caravaggio listing his contemporary artists in Rome by his categorisation of their capabilities. In a deposition during a 1603 libel case, he considered 'good artists' are those such as Gentileschi, Anibale Carracci and Federico Zuccaro[2]. Whether Caravaggio considered himself in this category remains speculation, but one would imagine he would. He merely states that these, what we might call today, 'A-listers', are the artists that talk to him and 'were his friends'.

Caravaggio is considered by many, a genius artist, certainly a celebrated artist, but only after hundreds of years of comparative neglect by scholars. Conversely, George Wombwell, not an artist of course, was considered a celebrity in his own life time, being extensively known across a wide representation of the British population. There would be few people that would not be able to describe Wombwell and his travelling menagerie of wild beasts and birds. Yet there are surprisingly few descriptions of him, probably just one or two illustrations, and after nearly two hundred years, it is us that have neglected George Wombwell and his famous travelling menagerie. The lack of contemporary documentation seems to have favoured Caravaggio more than Wombwell. Just a glimpse of Caravaggio's private life has led to a mountain of published scholarship. Caravaggio though, left a legacy of artwork on which much praise has been generated concerning the artist. In Wombwell's case, described often as 'the itinerant menagerist', there are very few lasting memories on which to rely. This makes the biographer's job a more erroneous task to establish scholarship. Today's extensive digitisation projects have assisted greatly in this respect, cutting timeframes from weeks to days and given resources such as the British Library, policies of wider digitisation of newspapers and journals over time, such research remains a moving target[3]. The continued uncovering of hitherto unknown references not available during the research phase of this biography, may make some of the book out of date in the future, but that can only be a good thing if it results in an even better understanding of George Wombwell and the life of the travelling menagerie.

The main sources of documentation up to 1825, are the many newspaper adverts undertaken on behalf of the travelling menagerie. In these, just the animal attractions are listed and very little is suggested on behalf of the showman. Unlike Caravaggio, whose artwork is celebrated today, George Wombwell was considered a celebrity in his own lifetime and it is us that have neglected his substantial influence on contemporary late Georgian and Victorian societies. Discovering new research has provided a greater understanding of the social history of late Regency Britain and on the notion of modern life.

During July 1825 a fight between a lion and 6 dogs was organised between George Wombwell the menagerist and the owners of the dogs. It was to be held at Warwick racecourse in the Midlands of England. This contest was extensively publicised prior to and reported after the event and was labelled shameful in these widespread newspaper reports. One commentator even called for the arrest of Wombwell over the issue. Conversely, other reports say these fights just did not occur and that it was simply a hoax. However, the expectation of excitement and the spectacle of a violent entertainment, if that is what it was, tended to outweigh the value of otherwise sensible newspaper reporting, or considered opinion, when it came to reporting some nineteenth century entertainments. The *Dictionary of National Biography* (1885), carries a description of the fight between two lions of Wombwell and dogs[4]. This is the definitive and lasting impression of Wombwell the man.

First published in 1885, it provides the populist view on George Wombwell's character, and many scholars have relied on its authenticity and have not ventured into the detail of the alleged event. Nor have they considered it in the wider context of late Georgian society. Given the previous lack of extensive research into Wombwell, it is not surprising that this view has remained today as the central characterisation of the Menagerist. This book investigates the historiography of the alleged Warwick event and considers what is true and what is myth. It will introduce new ideas, hitherto not seriously considered relevant to the event, and given this new evidence, makes informative arguments about the whole affair. I have researched the facts as they can be established today and, together with other available documentation from the early part of the nineteenth century, I have written this account of the *Events at Warwick*.

Background to the Lion and Dog Fight at Warwick

During the early part of 1825, provincial newspapers started to report an account of the intention for a fight between lions and dogs to be held at either Worcester or Warwick racecourses. These reports stated that the dogs had been chosen, their owners and the name of each dog listed. Other reports stated that the place chosen was Worcester but, after a few weeks, Warwick had been chosen. The latter had an arena in a factory yard converted to allow for an audience to watch the forthcoming event, some reports suggested. Yet other reports announced that the cage in which this fight was to take place was being constructed in Worcester, or even Shrewsbury. Finally, a report appeared that the cage had been completed and had arrived in Northampton on its way to Warwick.

This widespread publicity eventually reached the national papers, *The London Times* and *The Morning Chronicle* being the most influential at the time. Both papers repeated some of the aforementioned local news reports on the events at Warwick and this had led to widespread outrage about the forthcoming events. The following accounts are taken from a range of newspapers and periodicals around the country. It was possibly one of the most widely covered of event, other than those of international importance. It certainly would have assisted the sales of the papers, with an extensive and detailed coverage of the lion fight. Each report is an integral part of this book.

Reporting of The Lion Fight during the summer of 1825

The newspapers, both at national and provincial levels were full of accounts of how the build up to the fight gave rise to outrage and then of the fight itself. After the Warwick match, the reports turned to recrimination. Many of the reports are remarkably detailed in their descriptions including some of the less savoury aspects of a fight between dogs and lions, either real or imagined. The initial accounts include the following from *Jackson's Oxford Journal* on 2nd July 1825, that noted the following:

> The Lion Nero and the Dogs – Mr. Wombwell advertises that the grand combat between Nero, the great lion, and the dogs, will positively take place at Warwick, on the 26th July; the ground appointed is surrounded with high walls, on which seats will be erected – The Den has been removed from Shrewsbury to Northampton[5].

Jackson's Oxford Journal then reports on the 23rd July that 'the cage in which Mr. Wombwell intends this novel fight to take place, arrived in this borough on Wednesday last – *Warwick*

Paper'[6]. This had been quoted from a Warwick paper, but its title is not known. No less than seven newspapers carried the news of an impending fight on the 23rd July 1825, showing how the news had spread across the country.

Jackson's Oxford Journal on the 23rd and *The Examiner*, on the 24th, had, along with the announcement of the lion fight, carried a story of a bare knuckle fight, also at Warwick, between Jem Ward and Tom Cannon, where, according to the reports, 10,000 people watched Ward beat Cannon over ten rounds in very hot weather[7]. *The Examiner* account is very detailed in its description of this prize-fight. It starts:

> 'This combat took place on Tuesday, near Warwick, which 10,000 persons were present to witness, notwithstanding the extreme heat of the weather. Ten rounds only were fought, and from the beginning Cannon never had a chance of success. Of the two, if there was a choice, Ward stood up with the most determination – which was not expected. He had the best of the throwing, the best of the 'in-fighting', as the contest after 'closing' is termed, and absolutely won the battle in twelve minutes, without so much as a scratched face. Cannon

was hit hard, and hit a good deal; but certainly not enough to have beaten him if he had been in really good condition.'

It continues in this vain for many more lines of text and finally there is a comment on the so-called sport of prize fighting itself:

'The only result produced by it, as it seems to us, are, that it affords a pretence, a certain number of times in every year, for disturbing the peace of some country town, and filling it with riot and indecency; - secondly, that it furnishes besides, from time to time, the means of letting gentlemen of fortune expose themselves; - and lastly, that it supplies the means of existence, in idleness and vulgar luxury, to a whole horde of low gamblers, who are one of the first nuisances which the law of the country commonly exerts itself to abate. It can only be necessary for any person of decent habits to observe the style and demeanour of the individuals who systematically attend prize-fights, to be convinced – and here we by no means speak of the "operative" fighting men themselves – that those who thrive by such speculations are, at least, among the most unprofitable, not to say among the most offensive, members of the community – *Times*.'

In the same column, directly below this account, the *Examiner* lays out details of the anticipated lion fight. This report, *The Examiner* stated, had been taken from the *London Times*:

'In the course of Monday, Mr. Wombwell, the showman, arrived at Warwick with his lion, which is to be tortured for the public amusement on the 26th inst.; and a camel also came with him for the diversion of the idlers. The cage in which the 'Lion Fight' is to take place measures 15 feet in length by 14 feet in breadth, and is to be mounted upon a stage about six feet high. The lion is an extremely beautiful animal, and apparently is in good health as a beast kept constantly shut up in a caravan well may be. The arrangement now is that three dogs – not six – are to be set upon the poor creature at a time; but, whelped and bred as it has been in this country, and incessantly confined in a dark caravan without air or exercise, - how or by whom the dogs in question are to be furnished does not quite distinctly appear – but there can be very little question that the three dogs might be found, thirty times over, who would be more than a match for it; - and, indeed, the probability is, that a large bear, brought over at full length, would be a more formidable brute. From the comparatively confined extent of the cage which is to be used, the affair becomes more properly a 'bait', if we may draw distinctions in such a matter, than a 'fight', because there will be none of the open space, and consequent freedom of movement, which perhaps gave some sort of excitement to the same exhibitions when presented in a large arena. The poor creature who is to suffer all this horrible infliction is extremely tame; and allows his master freely to put his hands into the cage and caress him; and, whatever may be the curiosity (arising from its novelty) of such a spectacle, it is impossible to think of it but as a very depraved and wanton piece of cruelty – *Times.* '[8]

This report is also confirmed on the 25th July 1825 by the

Caledonian Mercury (Edinburgh, Scotland), once again being

placed below a report of the knuckle fight between Ward and

Cannon[9]. It reads:

'THE LION FIGHT

> This singular exhibition forms the next object of
> attraction to Warwick. The lion has arrived under the
> care of his owner, and a finer animal we have scarcely
> ever seen. He is upwards of five years of age, and was
> born in Scotland. The dogs by which he is to be fought,
> we understand, are of the bull dog breed and belong to
> some person in Liverpool, but to whom as well as the
> extent of the stakes yet remain a secret. The cage in
> which the fight is to take place has been erected in the
> factory yard. It is composed of a framework of wood, in
> which iron bars are inserted, and appears to be
> sufficiently strong. It is said Master Nero has been tried
> by dogs, and that he has not been found wanting in spirit
> and courage at the moment of attack. When caressed by
> Mr. Wombwell, however, he is as playful and as docile as
> a spaniel. Some doubts exist, however, whether the fight
> will be permitted to take place; but for these, Mr.
> Wombwell says, there is no foundation.'

The *Hampshire Telegraph and Sussex Chronicle etc.*

(Portsmouth, England), also reported on the 25th of July[10].

Although their article followed an account of the Ward/Cannon

match as well, it quickly became conflated within it. The paper

starts off under the heading 'FIGHT BETWEEN WARD AND

CANNON' describing the bare knuckle fight, but halfway through switches over to describing the build up to the lion fight.

In the course of Monday, Mr. Wombwell, the showman, arrived, with his Lion, which is to be tortured for the public amusement, on Tuesday the 26th inst. ; and a camel also came with him for the diversion of the idlers. The cage in which the " Lion Fight" is, to take place has been some days in Warwick in pieces, but will not be put together until the close of the week. It measures 15ft. in length by 14ft. in breadth, a dimension considerably less than by some mistake was originally stated ; and is to be mounted upon a stage, fixed upon wheels, about six feet high from the ground. Mr. Martin's information as to the condition of the lion, according to the description given by him some time back, does not seem to have been exactly correct. It is an extremely beautiful animal ; certainly not blind : and apparently in as good health as a beast kept constantly shut up in a caravan well may be. The arrangement now is, that three dogs—not six—are to be set upon the poor creature at a time ; but, whelped and bred as it has been in this country, and incessantly confined in a dark caravan without air or exercise,—how or by whom the dogs in question are to be furnished does not quite distinctly appear—but there can be very little question that three dogs might be found thirty times over who would be more than a match for it ; and, indeed, the probability is, that a large bear, brought over at full growth, would be a more formidable brute. From the comparatively confined extent of the cage which is to be used, the affair becomes more properly a " bait," if we may draw distinctions in such a matter, than a " fight," because there will be none of the open space, and consequent freedom of movement, which perhaps gave some sort of excitement to the same exhibitions when presented in a large arena. The poor

Hampshire Telegraph and Sussex Chronicle etc. (Portsmouth, England),

Monday, July 25, 1825; Issue 1346

creature who is to suffer all this horrible infliction is extremely tame, and allows his master freely to put his hands into the cage and caress him ; and, whatever may be the curiosity (arising from its novelty) of such a spectacle, it is impossible to think of it but as a very depraved and wanton piece of cruelty.

After the Lion was deposited, within his travelling caravan, in safety, preparations for accommodating the human exhibitors were set on foot. Several spots for fixing the stage were pitched upon, and upon one—a small close on the verge of the race-ground—it was actually erected. On the Tuesday morning, however, it became certain that the Mayor was in earnest, and would suffer no fighting where he could prevent it, and it became necessary, therefore, to look for a place which was out of his jurisdiction.

Hampshire Telegraph and Sussex Chronicle etc. (Portsmouth, England),
Monday, July 25, 1825; Issue 1346

The *Hampshire Telegraph* column then continued to describe the

erection of the Ward/Cannon fighting ring and the report of the

bare knuckle fight between Ward and Cannon. It carries on

eventually to discuss a SECOND FIGHT as an afterthought,

concerning 'Curtis, the pet of the Fancy… matched against Peter

Warren'. This was a description of another knuckle fighting

contest that occurred alongside that of the Ward/Cannon match. No further mention of Wombwell and his lion or the dogs is contained in this report. This mixing of events within one report is unusual compared to the other newspaper coverage. Although other newspapers had written about Ward and Cannon and then Wombwell, only the *Hampshire Telegraph* had conflated the two reports into one. It had also utilised a certain style in its reporting that we will return to later.

The next time that newspapers record anything about a Lion fight is a long and very descriptive and detailed account. It appeared on the 28th July 1825 in the prestigious *Morning Chronicle (London, England)[11]*. The following are the original newspaper columns published and confirms the date of the alleged event as Tuesday, July 26th 1825.

FIGHT BETWEEN THE LION NERO AND SIX DOGS, AT WARWICK.

This extraordinary exhibition, which has been so long announced, and upon which so much doubt has been thrown, took place on Tuesday evening, according to appointment. In our account of the late fight between Ward and Cannon, we stated that the Lion had actually arrived in Warwick, that the den in which the combat was to take place had been erected, and that there was every indication of Mr. Wombwell carrying his purpose into effect. Still the singularity of the spectacle was such, that a vast number of persons looked upon it as a mere hoax, and however anxious they might be to witness such a scene, they resolved not to run the hazard of disappointment. To this circumstance may be attributed the absence of many persons who would otherwise have flocked to the town.

Among other causes of doubt, was the whispered determination of the Mayor again to interpose his "brief authority," and to add to his unpopularity another petty interference with the wishes, or rather the interests of his townsmen; but this turned out to be altogether without foundation, for however willing he might be to do so ungracious a thing, the want of power rendered him harmless. It is true that he associated himself with Wheeler, Mr. Martin's Secretary, but after their joint research into ancient and modern Statutes, they were unable to discover one applicable to the case in question. The opinion of Mr. Allen, of Union Hall, was also taken, but he too was as much in the dark as the " wise men of Warwick," and could only refer to the Common Law authority for preventing a breach of the peace; an authority which, however it might apply to a fight between two men, had no reference to the approaching contest.

During the discussion, Mr. Wombwell went on steadily in making his arrangements, issued his bills, and prepared his tickets of admission, which were of various prices, from three sovereigns to half a sovereign.

The place chosen for the combat was the factory yard in which the first stage was erected for the fight between Ward and Cannon. This spot, which was, in fact, extremely well calculated for the exhibition, was now completely inclosed. We formerly stated that two sides of the yard were formed by high buildings, the windows of which looked upon the area, and the vacant spaces left were now filled up by Mr. Wombwell's collection of wild beasts, which were openly exposed, in their respective cages, on the one side, and by paintings and canvass on the other, so that, in fact, a compact square was formed, which was securely hidden from external observation. There was but one door of admission, and that was next the town. Upon the tops of the cages seats were erected, in amphitheatrical order; and for accommodation here, one guinea was charged. The higher prices were taken for the windows in the factories, and the standing places were 10s. each.

The Morning Chronicle (London, England) Thursday, July 28, 1825; Issue 1753

The centre of the square was occupied by the den—a large iron cage, the bars of which were sufficiently far asunder to permit the dogs to pass in and out, while the caravan in which Nero was usually confined, was drawn up close to it. The den itself was elevated upon a platform, fixed on wheels, about four feet from the ground, and an inclined plane formed of thick planks was placed against it, so as to enable the dogs to rush to the attack.

The dogs, six in number, arrived in Warwick as early as Friday last, and attracted a good deal of curiosity. They took up their quarters at the Green Dragon, where they held a levee, and a great number of persons paid sixpence each to have an opportunity of judging of their qualities, and certainly as far as appearance went, they seemed capable of doing much mischief. They were thus distinguished by names—1. Turk, a brown coloured dog.—2. Captain, a fallow and white dog, with skewbald face.—3. Tiger, a brown dog, with white legs.—4. Nettle, a little brindled bitch, with black head.—5. Rose, brindle-pied bitch.—6. Nelson, a white dog, with brindled spots.—One of them, Turk, had already been engaged in combat with another dog larger than himself, whom he had killed, and he bore a severe mark of punishment on the back of his head, which was almost scalped.

On Tuesday morning several persons were admitted to the factory to see the preparations, and at about ten o'clock the Dogs were brought in. They seemed perfectly ready to quarrel with each other, but did not evince any very hostile disposition either towards Nero, who, from his private apartment, eyed them with great complacency, or towards the other Lion and Lionesses by whom they were surrounded, and who, as it were, taunted them by repeated howlings, in which Nero joined chorus with his deep and sonorous voice. The dogs were in the care of a Mr. Edwards, John Jones, William Davis, and Samuel Wedgbury, a well-known dog-fancier in London. These persons said they were employed by the gentlemen who made the match; but the names of these gentlemen, if any such persons existed, were kept a "profound secret," although it was said, that no less a sum than 5,000l. depended upon the issue. With regard to Nero, a more beautiful or majestic animal has, perhaps, never been seen in this country. He seemed the very pride of his species, and there was a nobility and good nature on his countenance, which prepossessed every person in his favour; while it excited no small prejudice towards Mr. Wombwell, for exposing him to the danger, by which it was thought he was threatened; but Mr. Wombwell himself seemed to have very little doubt of the issue. Nero was stated to measure eleven feet from the tip of the nose to the end of the tail; and his proportions were in other respects large. He was five years of age in January last, was born in Edinburgh, and was so docile, as to permit his keeper to enter the den in which he was, and play with him with perfect safety. The cruelty of unnecessarily exposing such an animal to torture, naturally produced severe comments; and among other persons, a Quaker, being in the town of Warwick, waited upon Mr. Wombwell, on Tuesday morning, with the following letter, which he said he had received from a *friend* twenty miles from the town:—

The Morning Chronicle (London, England) Thursday, July 28, 1825; Issue 17533

" I have heard, with a great degree of horror, of an intended fight between a lion that has long been exhibited by thee, consequently has been long under thy protection, and six bull dogs. I seem impelled to write to thee on the subject, and to entreat thee, I believe in Christian love, that whatever may be thy hope of gain by this very cruel, and very disgraceful exhibition, thou wilt not proceed. Recollect that they are God's creatures, and we are informed, in the Holy Scriptures, that not even a sparrow falls to the ground without his notice; and as this very shocking scene must be to gratify a spirit of cruelty, as well as a spirit of gambling, for it is reported that large sums of money are wagered on the event of the contest, it must be marked with divine displeasure. Depend on it that the Almighty will avenge the sufferings of his tormented creatures on their tormentors—for though he is a God of love, he is also a God of justice, and I believe that no deed of cruelty has ever passed unpunished. Allow me to ask thee how thou wilt endure to see the noble animal thou hast so long protected, and which has been in part the means of supplying thee with the means of life, mangled and bleeding before thee. It is unmanly —it is mean and cowardly to torment any thing that cannot defend itself—that cannot speak to tell its pains and sufferings—that cannot ask for mercy. Oh! spare thy poor lion the pangs of such a death as may, perhaps, be his. Save him from being torn to pieces—have pity on the dogs that may as likely be torn by him. Spare the horrid spectacle—spare thyself the suffering that I fear will reach thee, if thou persist. Shew a noble example of humanity. Whoever has persuaded thee to expose thy Lion to the chance of being torn to pieces or of tearing other animals, are far beneath the brutes they torment—are unworthy the name of men, unworthy of being ranked among rational creatures. Suffer thyself to be entreated for thy own sake; whatever thou mayest gain by this disgraceful exhibition, will, I fear, prove like a canker-worm among the rest of thy substance. The writer of this most earnestly entreats thee to refrain from the intended evil, and to protect the animals in thy possession from all unnecessary suffering. The practice of benevolence will afford thee more true comfort, than the possession of thousands. Recommend the practice of benevolence to others, and always remember that He who gave life, did not give it to be ' the sport of cruel man,' and that he will assuredly call man to account for his conduct towards his dumb creatures. Remember also that

' Cowards are cruel, but the brave
Love mercy and delight to save.'

With sincere desire for the preservation of thy honour as a man of humanity, and for thy happiness and welfare every way, I remain thy friend, " S. HOARE."

However well meant this letter was—and that it arose in the purest motives of Christian charity no man could doubt,—with Mr. Wombwell it had no effect. He looked at his preparations—he looked at his Lion, and he cast a glance forward to his profits, and then shook his head. 'It must go on, said he—my Lion was challenged—he must fight. I am pledged to the public, and they must be gratified. The Quaker added his own mild and gentle and friendly entreaties; but it was in vain, and he left the Factory, in the consciousness, at least, of having done his duty, but with a heart heavy with regret that he had not succeeded.

The Morning Chronicle (London, England) Thursday, July 28, 1825; Issue 17533

Mr. Wombwell's trumpeters then went forth, mounted on horses, and in gaudy array, to announce the fight, which was fixed to take place between 5 and 7 in the evening. They travelled to Leamington, and the adjacent villages; but to have done good they should have gone still farther, for all who ventured from a distance on speculation, announced that those they left behind fully believed that their labour would be in vain.

With regard to the practice of Lions fighting with Dogs in this country, it has been in disuse for many years. Stow, in his Annals, gives the following account of a battle which took place between a Lion, and three Mastiffs, in the presence of James I. and his son Prince Henry.

"One of the dogs being put into the den, was soon disabled by the lion, who took him by the head and neck, and dragged him about. Another dog was then let loose, and served in the same manner; but the third being put in immediately, seized the lion by the lip, and held him for a considerable time; till being severely torn by his claws, the dog was obliged to quit his hold; and the lion, greatly exhausted by the conflict, refused to renew the engagement; but taking a sudden leap over the dogs, fled into the interior part of his den. Two of the dogs soon died of their wounds, the third survived, and was taken great care of by the prince, who said, 'he that had fought with the king of beasts, should never after fight with an inferior creature.'"

The Morning Chronicle (London, England) Thursday, July 28, 1825; Issue 17533

The *Morning Chronicle's* article formed the basis for many

other national and provincial reports about the Warwick event.

The *Liverpool Mercury (Liverpool, England)* on Friday, July 29,

1825 published a different, but as equally detailed account.

Although damaged it is worth inserting it here for comparison

with other reports.

FIGHT BETWEEN MR. WOMBWELL'S LION AND SIX BULL DOGS, FOR FIVE THOUSAND SOVEREIGNS!

"Accursed sports,
That owe their pleasure to another's pain."

It appears that the Magistrates have not, as was hoped and expected, succeeded in preventing the disgraceful and disgusting spectacle which took place at Warwick on Tuesday last. This is the more surprising, and less excusable, because the Attorney-General has given it as his opinion, that as the law now stands, any person wantonly maiming any animal, either by setting dogs at it or otherwise, is liable to transportation.

Independent of the wickedness of tormenting any creature for the amusement of man, we would ask what purpose, beyond that of brutalizing the spectators, can such scenes answer? If the combat at Warwick were intended as an experiment in natural history, to determine the relative power and courage of the lion and the dog, the result, in any case, would prove nothing. Hercules is said to have strangled serpents in his cradle; but this fabulous exploit is never looked upon as the *chef d'oeuvre* of that demi-god. The lion, which was so inhumanly tortured at Warwick, may be regarded as the infant Hercules: he has not attained, nor can he ever attain the prowess and activity that distinguishes the monarch of the forest in his state of nature. This poor beast, born in a cage in which he can scarcely turn himself, labouring under the effects of long and unnatural restraint and diet, is brought out to face a pack of fierce dogs, in the finest possible condition, both as to training and nourishment.

We record the description of the brutal spectacle with pain and loathing, as a disgraceful blot upon the national character; the details, disgusting as they are, will not be without their use, if they should stimulate the respectable part of the community to petition Parliament to prevent the repetition of such bestial exhibitions, if the law, as it now stands, is insufficient for their suppression.

The length of the following details obliges us to be much more brief in our commentary than the importance of the subject demands. They are supplied by an individual at Warwick, in whose playful style of treating the subject, under the assumption of the editorial cognomen, we by no means agree. The moral character of the age is deeply concerned in checking or eradicating that ferocious and unchristian spirit which appears to be alarmingly on the increase in this country. Hogarth's pencil was never more true to nature than in his celebrated series of pictures, illustrative of the progress of cruelty. His hero begins with tormenting dogs, cats, and inferior animals, and ends his career, by the murder of a fellow creature.

THE FIGHT.

Our readers are already in possession of the fact, that Mr. Wombwell has repeatedly declared, that he, some time ago, had made a match for the above sum, with a sporting gentleman whose name he was not authorized to make public, for his lion Nero to fight any six dogs of the bull breed he could produce. The conditions of the match were,—for three dogs to be set loose on the lion at the same time, and, in the event of one being destroyed by him, than another was to be set on ; so that he was not to be assailed by more than three dogs at one time. Nero, whose ancestors, no doubt, for a long succession of ages, were monarchs of their native wilds in Barbary, is not an exotic, but was brought forth in Scotland, and is not quite six years old. He is not, like the monster whose name he bears, a cruel and merciless tyrant, but a noble, majestic animal, mild and gentle in his manners, and remarkably obedient to his keepers. In fact, to the kind caresses of his master, Mr. Wombwell, who is exceedingly fond of him, he replies, with a grateful and benignant look, which speaks as plain as the *bow* of *Corporal Trim*, " your ho. nour is good." This, we believe, to be the true character of the lion Nero, who, although he exhibited, from his education, so much of the *suaviter in modo*, his master had little doubt but he possessed, also, so much of the *fortiter in re* as would enable him to be more than a match for his hardy opponents. Nero is in colour a fine beautiful tawny, approaching almost to a light chesnut, a mane fourteen inches long, the points ended with black, with a most commanding aspect, and upwards of four feet in height.

This singular combat took place on Tuesday, the 26th

The next columns of this 1825 report are damaged and not suitable for display. They can be examined at the British Library Newspaper Archives.

Continued:

The mob outside were exceedingly clamorous, and, before the contest ended, broke down the boards and rushed in by hundreds. Mr. Wombwell, in a most spirited manner, set about clearing the ground of the intruders, and, by the aid of a pretty good stick, which he applied very dexterously to the shoulders of many of them, succeeded beyond expectation. This business took up much time, and the payers began to call out, from different quarters, "Time! time!" The breach was pretty well made up, and men were stationed to keep out the mob.

The other three dogs were then brought out; on hearing them, Nero showed his uneasiness, by getting upon his legs, and going round the cage, evidently wishing to get away from the attack. These were stouter dogs than the first three. They rushed desperately in to him, and tried to fasten upon his nose; he beat them off as before, but with less effect; he seemed weaker, and ran to different parts of the cage to avoid them. They followed the lion up with the utmost fury, all seized him nearly together, and dragged him down. By a desperate effort he extricated himself, partially, but could not beat them off, and they brought him down a second time, when they were drawn.

The spectators were not satisfied with this proceeding, and insisted that one or the other should fairly be overcome. The dogs were then turned to him again, and brought Nero down to the floor twice more, by the nose and mouth; nor was he able to beat them entirely from their hold. The lion, however, made another effort, but he could not succeed, and they brought him down again, all having hold of his nose and mouth: the dogs were then drawn entirely off. Thus ended the combat. The fighting, at each time, lasted a quarter of an hour.

Nero, no doubt, beat the first three dogs, and, had there been no more, would have been decidedly the conqueror. But, by a succession of three fresh dogs, most of which would never have left off the attack till they had either been quite disabled, or destroyed, he was evidently overmatched. His mouth and nose must have been dreadfully lacerated, but he did not bleed much. The dogs were much torn about the head and neck, and bled profusely.

The prices of admittance were three guineas, two guineas, one guinea, and the standing places in the arena ten shillings. The company was numerous, but so many of them were in the buildings, we can form no correct idea of the sum taken at the doors. Had the prices been less, the place would have been filled to an overflow.

Liverpool Mercury etc. (Liverpool, England) on Friday, July 29, 1825

On the 30th July 1825, *Jackson's Oxford Journal (Oxford, England)* in their 'Postscript' section, made their own opinion public about the alleged events in Warwick[12].

THE LION FIGHT AT WARWICK.—We rejoice to observe the strong feeling of aversion with which the public in general have heard of this cruel exhibition. As a question of natural history, it may be deemed curious to ascertain the comparative ferocity of the lion and the bull-dog; but even in this respect the Warwick fight cannot be deemed satisfactory; for though the lion was a large and majestic animal, yet as he had been born and brought up in quite a domestic state, he had evidently little or nothing of the fury which a wild animal of the same species evinces in combat. Buffon observes that " the lion is very susceptible of the impressions given to him, and has always docility enough to be rendered tame to a certain degree." He adds, that " the lion, if taken young, and

Jackson's Oxford Journal (Oxford, England), Saturday, July 30, 1825; Issue 3770

brought up among domestic animals, easily ac-
customs himself to live with them, and even to
play without doing them injury: that he is
mild to his keeper, and even caressing, especially
in the early part of his life, and that if his natural fierceness now and then breaks out, it is
seldom turned against those who have treated
him with kindness." These remarks of the
great Naturalist are very fully confirmed by the
conduct of poor *Nero*, the animal so cruelly
tormented at Warwick; for both before and
after the combat he suffered·his keeper, Wombwell, with impunity, to enter his den, give him
water to drink, and throw the remainder over
his head.

Jackson's Oxford Journal (Oxford, England) Saturday, July 30, 1825; Issue 3770

Also included within the same *Jackson's Oxford Journal* issue,

was the lengthy and descriptive report that other newspapers had

published a few days earlier. *The Examiner (London, England)*

on the 31st of July, published the full description and credited the

Times of London for the article[13].

By the 6th of August 1825, this long report had been placed in at least the following newspapers:

Caledonian Mercury, Jackson's Oxford Journal, Bristol Mercury, Trewman's Exeter Flying Post and the *Plymouth and Cornish Advertiser* and *Ipswich Journal*, ensuring an almost blanket coverage across the country.

TO THE EDITOR OF THE TIMES.

Sir,—Having read in some of the London papers various false reports concerning the fight between *Nero* and the six dogs on Tuesday last, stating that he was torn, mangled, left in a pitiable condition, &c. &c., I must beg leave to contradict any such invidious representations. *Nero* was next morning exhibited to an immense concourse of visiters, anxious to see whether he was or was not much damaged; and, to their great astonishment, the noble animal showed no more signs of punishment than a few slight scratches on the lip. I was then induced by some friends to try the courage of my second lion, *Wallace*, whose natural disposition was not so much controlled by making so much freedom with him, or rendering him so tame, gentle, and submissive as was with *Nero*; and so the issue was, that *Wallace* quickly beat the six dogs sent at him, without receiving as much as a scar of the slightest description. There is also a talk of cruelty having been practised in the engagement. Now, Sir, can any man in his senses suppose that I would risk the loss of my two lions, the finest ever seen in this country, for the purpose of gratifying a cruel propensity? No, Sir, I never formed such an idea; and I further say that another exhibition of such a scene shall never be engaged in, or encouraged by, Sir, your most obedient servant.

Alcester, Aug. 1.   GEO. WOMBWELL.

On the 4th of August 1825, a letter appeared in *The London Times*, reportedly coming from George Wombwell[14].

A second letter, also purporting to be from George Wombwell appeared in the *Morning Post (London, England)* on the 5th August 1825. It read:

THE LATE LION FIGHTS.

TO THE EDITOR OF THE MORNING POST.

Worcester, August 3, 1825.

SIR—It is with astonishment I read in your Paper of Monday last, the statement of a Mr. WHEELER to the LORD MAYOR of London, of my determination in spite of his remonstrance to the contrary to proceed in the cruel, and as he termed it disgraceful exhibition of a second Lion Fight, that which took place on Saturday last, the 30th July. Who is this Mr. WHEELER? I never saw the man: he, nor any other person for him, never spoke to me concerning the prevention of such an exhibition: so far the contrary, I never had conversation with any Gentleman on the subject, who did not wish and encourage me to proceed in it. Accordingly I did so, without ever having the slightest hint from any person to prevent it.—But it is easier to prevent an evil than remedy it. Why did not Mr. WHEELER endeavour to prevent it before? Surely

The Morning Post (London, England) on the 5th August 1825

he and the public had timely notice of such a thing being about
to happen. Six months notice was given of it in the Newspapers, and why did not Mr. WHEELER speak before? Why
leave it to the last day, the last hour, nay, until it was all
over—as is the old adage, "After death the Doctor." Notwithstanding, was there any truth in his assertion, there would
be some excuse for him. His story of the Mayor of Warwick
is to me as astonishing as it is unfounded. The Mayor of Warwick or any other Magistrate never communicated to me any
intention on their part to prevent the combat. I never was in-
terrupted; the respectable inhabitants of Warwick were for,
not against its taking place. This Gentleman's statement is
really amazing: he says, he threatened me with not being allowed to exhibit in Bartholomew Fair. Good God! what an
unfounded assertion for a man who is so far famed for his
philanthropic and benevolent exertions in assisting Mr. MAR-
TIN in strictly enforcing the provisions of his Act for the Prevention of Cruelty to Animals. But I presume to hope, that
if Mr. WHEELER again states any thing of, or concerning this

The Morning Post (London, England) on the 5th August 1825

TO THE LORD MAYOR of London, his Lordship, or any other
Magistrate whom he shall trouble about it, will oblige him to
confirm his statement on oath; for if such reports as those fa-
bricated and published to my prejudice, are allowed to be circulated on the *bare word* of a person without having foundation
for doing so, no man's character can be safe. Indeed, there
came to me a Gentleman, a Mr. WHITEHEAD, I believe, a
member of that most respectable religious sect of people commonly called Quakers, about twelve o'clock on the morning
of the first combat, he very dispassionately and *without threats*,
told me, for his part he should not wish it to take place; but,
Mr. Editor, he came too late; all my preparations were made,
the Amphitheatre beginning to fill, and the tickets nearly all
disposed of. What was I to do, Sir, under such circumstances?
I was obliged to suffer it to go on, but not in that cruel outra-
geous disgraceful manner in which Mr. WHEELER described it;
quite the contrary. The Lions, both of them, are without
scratch or scar of any material injury, and the main object of
the second fight was, merely to shew what a difference there is
between a Lion in a tame state, and one in a savage state.—

The Morning Post (London, England) on the 5th August 1825

By giving this a place in your excellent Paper, you will do a kindness as well as an act of justice to
Sir, yours, with the greatest respect,
GEORGE WOMBWELL.

The Morning Post (London, England) on the 5th August 1825

Of course the most observant of us can see that the latter letter from Wombwell is post marked Worcester and dated the 3rd August 1825. The letter was published on the 5th August. The former letter from Wombwell is post marked Alcester (in Warwickshire) and is dated 1st August 1825. This letter was published on 4th August 1825. The distance between Worcester and Alcester is approximately 20 miles, although, according to maps of the time, it would have been quite a direct route between the two towns. I can see some continuity between the two documents on the basis of location alone, given 20 miles was easily achievable for a horse-drawn travelling show via the 1825 road system. However, I am not convinced either letter was from George Wombwell, but were sent in by some other person or persons, maybe having been provoked to do so by their own objections to the alleged fight.

Both letters were signed off differently, 'your most obedient servant' and 'yours with the greatest respect' respectively. In the first letter Wombwell says 'having read in some of the London papers', but would someone in Alcester have the London papers to hand during 1825? Both letters contained details that could have been copied verbatim from previously published newspaper reports and the styles are also quite different. However, the reader must make their own minds as to the validity of each letter.

Further Fallout from the Lion Fight

Fallout continued to befall Wombwell after the widespread reports of the lion fight at Warwick. On the 20th August 1825, the *Caledonian Mercury (Edinburgh, Scotland)* published an account of a menagerist known as Messrs James's. The report referred to Wombwell as an 'example' in a report that James was about to match a 'Bonassus' (probably an American Bison), against a 'certain number of dogs'[15]. He was stopped on his route to Exeter, the report continues, by a farmer who wagered his mastiff dog against the beast for the sum of £5 against a heifer should the dog be unsuccessful. The dog failed, according to the report, and the farmer lost his heifer. 'Mr Wombwell's example, it seems, is likely to form a precedent for similar exhibitions' stated the journal, clearly blaming Wombwell for this rise in wagers on fighting animals.

The Morning Chronicle (London, England) on Tuesday, September and *The Caledonian Mercury (Edinburgh, Scotland)* on Saturday, 10th of September, 1825, continued to publicise Wombwell in a bad light with articles reporting on an appearance by George Wombwell at a Magistrates court in London[1617]. Wombwell, it states, was charged with the assault of a respectable tradesman named Att from Southwark. Wombwell appeared before Mr R J Chambers at Union Hall, which held appearances before the Magistrates for the county of Surrey. In court Att stated that he had gone to Wombwell's Menagerie at Peckham (Camberwell in the *Caledonian Mercury* report) and enquired of the two lions, Wallace and Nero. Mrs Wombwell, acting as cashier, had told Att the lions were indeed in the Menagerie that day and the plaintive paid the entrance fee to see them.

After seeing Nero, he observed a man, whom he thought was about to feed the lion, and was taken to follow other spectators to get a closer look. In doing so, Att stated, he had inadvertently joined a queue for the exit and was taken outside the exhibition area, not having seen Wallace. He then endeavoured to return inside, but was barred from doing so by Wombwell, he had claimed. Att

explained that he had exited by mistake and was assuming that Wombwell would let him back inside. He attempted to push past Wombwell, whom he said immediately seized him 'by the collar' and called to other persons, whom Wombwell had instructed to give the plaintiff a beating. Wombwell denied attacking the man, but did admit that his men had assaulted Mr Att. Att was eventually released and driven out of the Menagerie.

Att went to the original entrance again and on recognition by Mrs Wombwell was allowed back into the Menagerie. He said he then asked Mr Wombwell for an apology. The reply apparently was that he, Wombwell had lost L.50 [50 pounds] last year at Bartholomew Fair by people rushing at the exit without paying and he was determined not to permit entrance through it again. Att then added that Wombwell also stated that he was not accountable for the actions of his men, who, the plaintiff added, were intoxicated. Att then continued his visit to the Menagerie and then went away, seeing that he was not going to get any apology from Wombwell. The following morning, he obtained the court warrant against Wombwell, but not the other man, since at that time he did not know the name of the man that he claimed had struck him. Mr Wombwell was asked the name and he replied that it had been one George Haines.

The Magistrate ordered a warrant to be issued against Haines and called upon Wombwell to produce 'two respectable housekeepers (who immediately appeared) to answer the charge' at the session. His Worship said that Mr Wombwell's conduct towards the plaintiff, was as bad as his treatment towards his wild beasts, Wombwell having held Att's arms to prevent him from defending himself. This rather confusing ending to the report concerning 'housekeepers' leads me to believe it was not correctly reported, but the direct reference to the lion fight was obviously a way a Magistrate could make sure that Wombwell knew of his dissatisfaction over the events at Warwick. I suspect the report should have stated that two men from Wombwell's menagerie were to be brought before the Magistrates and that Wombwell himself, was not actually involved in the fracas at the exit of the exhibition at all. There was no verdict reported against Wombwell or his men in these accounts. Wombwell was in the London area for the annual Bartholomew Fair held each year in Smithfield Market area of the city and this had not escaped the newspapers either.

Berrow's Worcester Journal (Worcester, England), on Thursday, September 08, 1825 had the following short insertion[18]:

> **Wombwell has a very conspicuous situation in Bartholomew Fair;** the public indignation against him has, it seems, so far subsided, that no obstruction has been offered to his occupying a booth with his " noble *hanimals as fowt the dogs at Varrick.*"

It had been thought, according to newspaper reports, that the events of Warwick would enrage the authorities responsible for

Bartholomew Fair in London's Smithfield so much that they would deny Wombwell access to the fair. *The Morning Chronicle (London, England)* on the 30th July 1825 reported that 'the second battle would certainly take place, if the Chief Magistrate of the City of London did not refuse Wombwell the advantage he had been accustomed to enjoy at Bartholomew Fair'[19]. Wheeler, the agent of the Society for the Prevention of Cruelty to Animals had drawn to the attention of the Lord Mayor of London, the events at Warwick claiming the prospect of a second lion fight. Wheeler had gone to Warwick according to the report, to 'endeavour to prevent the fight between the lion Nero and the six dogs, by procuring Magistraterial interference'. This application had been declined however, and he was appearing before the Lord Mayor in order that some pressure be placed on Wombwell to prevent the second fight, which Wheeler must have originally heard about via newspaper reports sometime between the 25th July 1825 and the morning of the 30th July 1825, the date of the published report of his appearance before the Lord Mayor of London concerning Bartholomew

Fair. Of course, Wombwell in his letter of the 3rd August stated that he had never heard of Mr Wheeler and had never spoken to him about the events at Warwick. This later report continues 'the Lord Mayor said, he had no power to interfere in the case' and had no powers to influence a Warwick Magistrate on the matter. Wheeler still insisted that the Lord Mayor could halt the second fight, but the Lord Mayor declined to become involved in the matter.

Wombwell in his letter of the 3rd August, did however, state that a Mr Whitehead came to him to have the fight cancelled. In the report on the 28th July, it was claimed Whitehead had handed Mr Wombwell a letter 'from a friend 20 miles from the town[20]. The content of that letter was reproduced as part of the *Morning Chronicle (London, England)* report of the 28th July 1825. 'S. Hoare' was the name at the bottom of this letter, according to the report, and Hoare had appealed to Wombwell's better nature thus:

'The practice of benevolence to others, and always remember

that *He* who gave life, did not give it to be *the sport of cruel men*, and that he will assuredly call man to account for his conduct towards his dumb creatures.' Hoare signs off 'With sincere desire for the preservation of thy honour a man of humanity'

Notwithstanding this concern, on the 2nd of August 1825 the *Morning Chronicle (London, England)* had already carried a report under the headline 'Second Grand Fight at Warwick'[21]. It proceeded in the same style to provide a very detailed description of a fight between the lion Wallace this time, and the dogs, now given names as Tinker, Ball, Sweep, Turpin, Billy and Tiger. It appeared therefore, that whilst Whitehead was appealing to have the contest banned, it had, claimed the newspaper reports, already taken place. The date of such a contest is not stated, but it must have been after the 26th of July, the date of the first contest and had happened, if at all, between the Sunday 27th July and the 1st August, given the report appeared on the 2nd of August 1825.

SECOND GRAND FIGHT AT WARWICK, BEWEEN THE LION WALLACE, A SCOTTISH HERO, AND SIX DOGS.—THE LION VICTORIOUS.

In our Paper of Saturday we stated that immediately after the match between Nero and his six opponents, a fresh match was made between a second Lion, called Wallace, and six other Dogs. It was stated that this match was made for a hundred pounds aside; but without waiting to inquire into the motives of the exhibition, we shall proceed to describe the fight, as it took place, which becomes the more interesting as the Lion bravely vindicated the character of his species, by conquering his opponents.

Wallace, like Nero, was born in Edinburgh, but it would seem that he came from a different stock, and was naturally of a more ferocious and untractable disposition. From his earliest infancy, he was wild and unmanageable in his habits, and resented the familiarity of his keepers, unless when in a particularly good humour, with great tenacity. He was born in September, 1819, and his weight is calculated at 400 pounds, about 100 pounds less than Nero. To all appearance his strength was not equal to that of Nero, but in spirits and determination there was no comparison.

The fight took place in the Factory-yard, as before, and the preparations were precisely similar. In the course of the morning Wallace was removed into a caravan, so as to be brought close to the den where he remained the whole of the day. The prices of admission were reduced to five shillings, and half-a-crown each person, but even at this rate the numbers present were comparatively few. Indeed the tameness with which the former fight went off, led to a belief that the present exhibition would have been equally uninteresting.

As the spectators arrived, they of course made anxious inquiries as to the state of Nero, who was exposed to view, and appeared little the worse for his late battle. There were a few scars on his nose and lips, but nothing of any importance. His general health was good, and he evinced the same docility of disposition by which he has always been distinguished. From Nero the curious turned to the dogs, by whom he had been opposed, and it turned out, as we anticipated, that the gallant Turk, whose game was so conspicuous in the first assault, had paid the forfeit of his life to his bravery. The injuries he received in his battle with his brother bull dog, added to those sustained from his repeated attacks on the lion, were such as to forbid the hope of recovery, and he died on the Thursday. Of the remaining five, Nettle, the brindled bull bitch, has been sold at a high price, and the other four have not yet recovered from the wounds which they received. They still remain in the factory under the care of their owners.

The dogs intended for the battle with Wallace were in the same room with the invalids, and looked extremely well. They were named for the occasion, and were either bulls or half bred, between bull and mastiff. They were called Tinker, Ball, Sweep, Turpin, Billy, and Tiger.

It was nearly 8 o'clock before Wallace was turned into the den —a ceremony which was not quite so easily performed as with Nero. He immediately ran round his new apartment with a spirit and activity which shewed that he was perfectly at ease. His head was erect, and he lashed his sides with his tail in such a manner as convinced the spectators that he did not intend to "play light" with his antagonists. It was agreed that two dogs should be let slip at a time, and that twenty minutes should be allowed the Lion between each assault. Umpires were, in this case regularly appointed. Mr. Phillips, of Shrewsbury, for Mr. Wombwell, and Mr. Rainford, of Liverpool, for the Dogs. Edwards and Wedgbury handled the dogs.

The Morning Chronicle (London, England)

Tuesday, August 2, 1825; Issue 17537

THE FIGHT.

At a given signal Tinker and Ball were led, in their collars, to the platform, and as they approached began to bark with great vociferation, as well as to shew an anxious disposition to commence the attack. Wallace, the moment he heard them, turned round in the direction in which they were coming, and, as if conscious that mischief was meant towards himself, he watched their progress, with his head erect, his tail stiff, and his whole appearance indicating courage and resolution. At last the dogs came in his front, and he had them in full view. He approached close to the bars, and boldly waited their attack. The collars were at last slipped, and both dogs rushed in together. Wallace stepped back a pace, and at the moment Tinker jumped at his nose, he caught him like a rat between his teeth, while he pushed Ball off with one of his paws, and for a moment held him on the floor. He then walked off with Tinker in the most majestic manner, while he treated with contempt the renewed efforts of Ball, to seize his under lip, and occasionally pushed him off with his claws. After holding Tinker in his mouth for two minutes, during which time he nearly made his teeth meet in his body, he let him drop, as if satisfied with his vengeance. The moment Tinker found himself at liberty, he thought it convenient to retire, and crawled out of the den perfectly satisfied that " the better part of valour is wisdom." He was immediately carried to the infirmary in a pitiable state. Ball, undismayed by the fate of his companion, continued to rush to the Lion's head; and at last shared the same fate with Tinker. Wallace seized him by the neck, and walked about with him, growling like a cat with a mouse in its mouth, till Wedgbury luckily caught hold of him by the leg, and dragged him through the bars dreadfully lacerated. Thus ended the first assault, and so convinced were the spectators, that the dogs would be second best, that two to one were offered on the Lion. Wallace having thus got rid of his first assailants, walked about with great dignity; looking in all directions as if he expected a fresh attack. He was in no respect distressed, but still the stipulated time was permitted to elapse before the

SECOND ASSAULT.

At the end of the twenty minutes, Turpin, a London dog, and Sweep, a native of Liverpool, were brought forth, and their approach was announced by loud barking. Wallace pricked up his ears, and looked round with perfect confidence. The dogs having been brought to the platform, they renewed their barking and howling; and Wallace being thus satisfied of the point at which he was to be attacked, deliberately approached the platform as close as he could, and seating himself on his haunches, fixed his eyes on the dogs with a most terrific glare. He watched them precisely as a cat would watch a mouse, which it expected to dart from a hole. The word, " let go," having been given, the dogs rushed upon their fate; and, in less than a minute, were disposed of. Turpin made the first spring, and Wallace instantly caught him in his formidable jaws, giving him a most unseemly scrunch. The attack of Sweep now induced Wallace to drop Turpin, and turn to his new opponent, on which Turpin crawled out with all possible celerity. Sweep next had his allowance, Wallace seized him with both his claws, and was about to give him a crack between his jaws, when he luckily made a spring and bolted out of the den. Some of the spectators suggested that Sweep ought to have another run; but the umpires decided otherwise, and indeed we think it would have required more than ordinary inducements to persuade Sweep to renew the attack.

The Morning Chronicle (London, England)

Tuesday, August 2, 1825; Issue 17537

THIRD ASSAULT.

Wallace again had a clear stage, and as a reward for his valour, one of his keepers threw him a paunch, which he devoured with as much *gout* as an Alderman would eat a basin of turtle. In fact, he was quite undisturbed by his labours, and evidently regarded them as mere pastime. A consultation was now held between Wedgbury and Edwards as to the expediency of exposing the third pair of dogs to certain destruction. Wedgbury was decidedly averse to the attempt, the more especially as his own dog Billy, a very fine white bull, about eighteen months old, was booked for the affray. Edwards, less squeamish, led forth Tiger towards the platform. Wedgbury scratched his head and said, "he know'd as his dog would be killed—it was no use," and then he cast a look of mortification at the wounded and dying by which he was surrounded. Edwards called out "come along," and Wedgbury followed, as if he were himself about to be baited. There was some talk about "disappointing the gemmen," but Wedgbury thought this was of little importance, compared with the loss of what he called "one of the best dogs in England." At last certain threats were held out which overcame his scruples, and both dogs were led to the scratch, much less affected by their situation than their masters. Wallace, on hearing the barkings of his fresh customers, rose up and again faced the platform. He placed himself so near the bars of the den, that the dogs could not get fairly in to the attack, and he was therefore driven back, but he returned nearly to the same position. Billy was first let go, and being the largest as well as the most courageous dog, Wallace seemed to fancy him for his first victim, and the instant he came within reach, he grasped him across the loins with his jaws, and lifting him up, walked off with as much ease as if he carried a *cockchafer*. The moment Tiger witnessed this unexpected feat, he looked perfectly astounded, and with a rapidity quite equal to his entrance, he turned about, shrugged his shoulders, and took to his trotters, prudently declining any further acquaintance with such an "out-and-outer." Wedgbury, who was in greater agony than his dog, exclaimed against having been gammoned to risk him, and seizing an opportunity, he caught Billy by the leg, and drew him out of the den, severely wounded, by the eye-teeth or tusks of Wallace on both sides.

Thus terminated the second fight, apparently to the satisfaction of all parties, who seemed to be highly delighted, that the noble Wallace had been victorious.

Most of the dogs are in a dangerous state; and we have no doubt that this lion would be a match for any six dogs that might be opposed to him. There was no attempt on the part of the Magistrates to interrupt the exhibition, which Mr. Wombwell describes upon the whole as having been unprofitable.

The Morning Chronicle (London, England)

Tuesday, August 2, 1825; Issue 17537

The Morning Post on Wednesday 10th August 1825, published the meeting of the City Lands Committee, which had taken place on the previous Saturday[22]. This meeting included the 'taking into consideration that of letting the grounds in Smithfield to the several applicants for situations in which to erect buildings for the exhibition of pantomimers, interludes, giants, dwarfs, wild beasts &c.' By this time Bartholomew Fair had irritated many members of the Committee and efforts to have it abolished were already common at these meetings. In addition to the usual complaints about 'excesses of drinking and other kinds of debauchery' the report ends with a comment on George Wombwell:

> 'It is whispered that Mr Wombwell will be denied the opportunity of exhibiting poor Nero and Wallace, as his conduct has excited the utmost disgust in the City.'

As we already know, Wombwell still attended Bartholomew Fair that year and neither the Lord Mayor nor the Lands Committee had been convinced enough to bar Wombwell from appearing with his wild beasts at the Fair.

On the 15th August 1825, *The Morning Post* reported that
Wombwell was on the road to London and that as a consequence
'of the false reports recently published in the newspapers of the
cruelty practiced by Mr. Wombwell he would 'exhibit them
around the metropolis, in order to convince the public that such
reports were groundless; the Lions are without scar or blemish,
they are healthy, lively, whole, and strong as ever they were.'[23]

Yet another report of the Surrey Session was published in *The
Bury and Norwich Post, (Bury Saint Edmunds, England,* this
tima as late as Wednesday, November 09, 1825[24]. This report
claimed it was the Peckham Fair and that Wombwell had 'held
him tight' being 'a powerful man' whilst one of the keepers,
came up and stuck him several times severely in the face.
However, it continues in a more conciliatory manner towards
Wombwell on the affair. It states that 'the prosecutor [Att] was
very obstreperous and in liquor' at the time of the said offence.
Stains, one of Wombwell's servants, who was also intoxicated, it
claimed, came up and struck Mr Ott [Att] several times. It

reported that 'Mr Wombwell was very angry, and said he would discharge him for his misbehaviour' and that Wombwell made use of no violence. He had, the report stated, 'simply put his open hand on Mr Ott's back'. Feltham, a servant of Mr Wombwell, deposed that Stains was discharged the morning after the assault, for his violence the preceding evening[25]. The Chairman, 'having summed up the evidence, the Jury returned a verdict of Not Guilty'.

So there was clearly plenty of fallout from the reporting of the events at Warwick. Outside the scope of the national newspapers, another journal also made reference to the events. William Hone (1780 – 1842), a significant figure in 19th century London culture, especially the printed word, produced a publication between the years 1825 – 27, titled *The Every-Day Book*[26]. Presented in the form of an almanac, a number of pages were given over to July 26th 1825 and contain a very detailed description of the events at Warwick to include a republication of several newspaper reports.

An etching accompanied Hone's entry, which had been copied from one of the various newspaper accounts, in this case *The Morning Herald*. With dogs attacking the lion's face, it had clearly been inspired by the newspaper reports[27].

Tame Lion Bait.

"The dogs would not give him a moment's respite, and all three set on him again, while the poor animal howling with pain, threw his great paws awkwardly upon them as they came."
Morning Herald.

Excerpt from Hone's *Every-Day Book* for 1825

Mr. Hoare's excellent letter, with the particulars of this brutal transaction, thus far, are from *The Times* newspaper which observes in its leading article thus:

" With great sincerity we offered a few days ago our earnest remonstrance against the barbarous spectacle then preparing, and since, in spite of every better feeling, indulged—we mean the torture of a noble lion, with the full consent, and for the profit, of a mercenary being, who had gained large sums of money by hawking the poor animal about the world and ex- hibiting him. It is vain, however, to make any appeal to humanity where none exists, or to expatiate on mercy, justice,

Excerpt from Hone's *Every-Day Book* for 1825

and retribution hereafter, when those whom we strive to influence have never learned that language in which alone we can address them.

" Little more can be said upon this painful and degrading subject, beyond a relation of the occurrence itself, which it was more our wish than our hope to have prevented. Nothing, at least, could be so well said by any other person, as it has by a humane and eloquent member of the Society of Friends, in his excellent though unavailing letter to Wombwell. What must have been the texture of that mind, on which such sentiments could make no impression?"

This question may be illustrated by Wombwell's subsequent conduct.

Excerpt from *Hone's Every-Day Book* for 1825

> and though well aware of the impropriety of doubting the authority of the keeper of the menagerie, we must admit that our impression is, that no match was made, that no wagers were laid, and that the affair was got up for the laudable purpose hinted at in the commencement of this notice.

Excerpt or *Hone's Every-Day Book* for 1825

Hone had therefore not edited the reports to his advantage it seems, given he published the *Morning Herald* (undated) account which also called into question whether the fights ever took place as shown in the example above[28]

The Every-Day Book published an entry for 5th September where Hone provided an extended coverage of the history of Bartholomew Fair delving into its roots, but more importantly, he describes the shows that appeared at the fair during 1825 including Wombwell's menagerie as follows:

SHOW XXII.

WOMBWELL.

The back of this man's menagerie abutted on the side of the last show, and ran the remaining length of the north-side of Smithfield, with the front looking towards Gilt-spur-street; at that entrance into the Fair it was the first show. This front was entirely covered by painted show-cloths representing the animals, with the proprietor's name in immense letters above, and the words "The Con-quering Lion" very conspicuous. There were other show-cloths along the whole length of the side, surmounted by this inscription, stretching out in one line of large capital letters, "NERO AND WALLACE; THE SAME LIONS THAT FOUGHT AT WARWICK." One of the front show-cloths represented one of the fights; a lion stood up with a dog in his mouth, crunched between his grinders; the blood ran from his jaws; his left leg stood upon another dog squelched by his weight. A third dog was in the act of flying at him ferociously, and one, wounded and bleeding, was fearfully retreating. There were seven other show-cloths on this front, with the words "NERO AND WALLACE" between them. One of these show-cloths, whereon the monarch of the forest was painted, was inscribed, "Nero, the Great Lion, from Caffraria!"

The printed bill described the whole collection to be in "fine order." Six-pence was the entrance money de-manded, which having paid, I entered the show early in the afternoon, although it is now mentioned last, in con-formity to its position in the Fair. I had experienced some inconvenience, and witnessed some irregularities incident to a mixed multitude filling so large a space as Smithfield; yet no disorder without, was equal to the dis-order within Wombwell's. There was no passage at the end, through which persons might make their way out: perhaps this was part of the proprietor's policy, for he might imagine that the universal disgust that prevailed in London, while he was manifesting his brutal cupidity at Warwick, had not subsided; and that it was necessary his show-place here should appear to fill well on the first day of the Fair, lest a report of general indifference to it, should induce many persons to forego the gratification of their curiosity, in accommodation to the natural and right feeling that induced a determination not to enter the exhibition of a man who had freely submitted his animals to be tortured. Be that as it may, his show, when I saw it, was a shameful scene. There was no person in attendance to exhibit or point out the animals[.] They were arranged on one side only, and I made my way with difficulty towards the end, where a loutish fellow with a broomstick, stood against one of the dens, from whom I could only obtain this information, that it was not his business to show the beasts, and that the showman would begin at a proper time. I patiently waited, expecting some announcement of this person's arrival; but no intimation of it was given; at length I discovered over the heads of the unconscious crowd around, that the showman, who was evidently under the influence of drink, had already made his way one third along the show. With great difficulty I forced myself through the sweltering press somewhat nearer to him, and managed to get opposite Nero's den, which he had by that time reached and clambered into, and into which he invited any of the spectators who chose to pay him sixpence each, as many of them did, for the sake of saying that they had been in the den with the noble animal, that Wombwell, his master, had exposed to be baited by bull-dogs. The man was as greedy of gain as his master, and therefore without the least regard to those who wished for general information concerning the different animals, he maintained his post as long as there was a prospect of getting the sixpences. Pressure and heat were now so excessive, that I was compelled to struggle my way, as many others did, towards the door at the front end, for the sake of getting into the air. Unquestionably I should not have entered Wombwell's, but for the purpose of describing his exhibition in common with others. As I had failed in obtaining the information I sought, and could not get a printed bill when I entered, I re-ascended to endeavour for one again; here I saw Wombwell, to whom I civilly stated the great inconvenience within, which a little alteration would have obviated; he affected to know nothing about it, refused to be convinced, and exhibited himself, to my judgment of him, with an understanding and feelings perverted by avarice. He is undersized in mind as well as form, "a weazen, sharp-faced man," with a skin reddened by more than natural spirits, and he speaks in a voice and language that accord with his feelings and propensities. His bill mentions, "A remarkably fine tigress in the same den with a noble British lion!!" I looked for this companionship in his menagerie, without being able to discover it[29].

Hone is less than flattering towards Wombwell, with the curious comment concerning him:

'undersized in mind as well as form, "a weazen, sharp-faced man," with a skin reddened by more than natural spirits, and he speaks in a voice and language that accord with his feelings and propensities '.

This, in my view, more than any other historical document has provided a lasting characterisation of George Wombwell the person, for over two centuries. The impression given is of a man of short stature, a thin, but pointed and shrivelled face. A thinly veiled notion of intoxication, given Hone's use of the phrase 'a skin reddened by more than natural spirits' is worthy of anything that Charles Dickens might have penned about one of his characters, a decade or two later.

Hone also describes the menagerie as he faces the Wombwell pitch at the Fair:

> *There were other show-cloths along the whole length of the side, surmounted by this inscription, stretching out in one line of large capital letters, "NERO AND WALLACE; THE SAME LIONS THAT FOUGHT AT WARWICK." One of the front show-cloths represented one of the fights; a lion stood up with a dog in his mouth, crunched between his grinders; the blood ran from his jaws; his left leg stood upon another dog squelched by his weight. A third dog was in the act of flying at him ferociously, and one, wounded and bleeding, was fearfully retreating. There were seven other show-cloths on this front, with the words "NERO AND WALLACE" between them. One of these show-cloths, whereon the monarch of the forest was painted, was inscribed, "Nero, the Great Lion, from Caffraria!"*

Print of Mary Ellen Best, ,*Caravans in Peasholme, York*, 1833,
George Wombwell Collection

He refers to the presence of 'show-cloths'. As you can see from

the 1833 painting by Mary Ellen Best, show-cloths were indeed

used by Wombwell, on his caravan walls. The painted wooden

caravans we have become used to seeing in late Victorian and

Edwardian photographs, were not present in 1825. It was left to

loose cloths being decorated as required and then suspended

over the sides of the caravans that made up the menagerie booth.

It is feasible, indeed likely, that Wombwell would advertise the

events at Warwick even if they had not taken place.

Wombwell was not averse to publicity, and anything that attracted spectators to his booth rather than those of his competitors, would be likely to be utilised. It seems to me to be the equivalent to the modern day 'Freddie Starr Ate My Hamster' moment![30]

A front page article appeared in *The Sun,* a British tabloid newspaper, on March 13th 1986 allegedly suggesting a popular British comedian of the time, Freddie Starr, had placed a hamster in a sandwich after the owner of the pet refused to make him a snack. 'He put my hamster between two slices of bread and started eating it,' she said, 'I was sickened and horrified'. The animal's owner, Lea La Salle, allegedly claimed that Starr had killed the hamster. After the immense publicity around the event the comedian's publicist, Max Clifford, giving evidence at the 2012 Leveson Enquiry into media ethics, admitted he had given permission for *The Sun* newspaper to run the story even though it was probably not true.

Wombwell's own 'hamster moment' gave rise to increased publicity for his menagerie, with an accompanying increase in attendances, and, knowing that he would soon be at the annual Bartholomew Fair, had, according to Hone's report, advertised the lion and dog fight in large headline lettering:

'NERO AND WALLACE; THE SAME LIONS THAT FOUGHT AT WARWICK'

The practice of painting cloth would be a quick and economic way of advertising the menagerie's contents, such as the 'Wild Boar' and other signs in Best's painting. It would be particularly useful where the availability of wild beasts was prone to fluctuate given the short lifespan of some animals kept in captivity in the early nineteenth century. One sign could be removed and a new one placed as new animals arrived from the new world.

Hone completes his description of Bartholomew Fair by making a statement which echoes Wheeler, the agent of the Society for the Prevention of Cruelty to Animals to the Lord Mayor and the

Lands Committee.

> 'Bartholomew Fair must and will be put down. It is for this reason that so much has been said of its former and present state. No person of respectability now visits it, but as a curious spectator of an annual congregation of ignorance and depravity'[31]

It's hard to know exactly what had concerned Hone other than his apparent contempt for such violence between animals, but his vitriolic attack on Wombwell's character is rather curious. However, it is more likely to be concerned with getting Bartholomew Fair banned. Wombwell may have been merely a pawn in the political in-fighting with the local authorities that had the power to sanction the Fair's running each year. It may be interesting to know that one of Hone's printing premises was in Ludgate Hill, just a few hundred yards from the hustle and bustle of Bartholomew Fair when it was in full flight. However, by the time of the 1825 Fair, Hone had already been lodged in a debtor's prison and, after some of his friends came to his rescue, he established himself in a coffee house in Gracechurch Street, in the heart of the City of London. Being a debtor, after running what Hone must have hoped to be a successful printing

company, might have antagonised the situation of also living and

working nearby to the Fair, and he likely became quite jealous

of Wombwell's success as a businessman. This could have given

further impetus to his verbal attack on Wombwell's character.

Hone's *Every-Day Book* and his other publications during the

late 1820s were not very successful, hence his time spent in the

debtor's prison after becoming bankrupt[32]. In 1821 Hone

published a text – *The Political Showman at Home* in which he

satirises several political characters. Accompanied by drawings

from George Cruikshank each 'animal' is described in some

detail as to its character. One such entity is the *Bloodhound* or

Ban Dog[33]. This is described thus:

> 'When it scents a human victim it follows his track with
> cruel perseverance, flies upon him with dreadful ferocity,
> and, unless dragged off, tears and rends the form until
> every noble feature of humanity is destroyed.'

It seems to me that Hone may have had this in mind when he set

about destroying George Wombwell's character.

All this time though, Bartholomew Fair flourished, even with the continuing barrage of newspaper published criticism concerning its poor reputation. George Wombwell, meanwhile, remained the 'the star' of the fair according to George Cruikshank the satirist and cartoonist[34]. 'The Hyperion of the fair – it [Wombwell's Booth] stood out bright and undaunted as in happier times – it was the last gallant upholder of poor Smithfield's dying splendour', writes George Cruikshank in an article 'A Peep at Bartholomew Fair' from his book *George Cruikshank's Omnibus* of 1842. Clearly, Cruikshank hints at the demise of the fair, which did eventually fold after 1854 when the City Corporation suppressed any further proclamations for being 'one of London's most raucous entertainments'[35]. However, in 1842 George Wombwell is still seen in good light despite the growing poor reputation of the Fair.

Legislation and the Society for the Prevention of Cruelty to Animals (SPCA)

I now turn to what else was happening during a period when the events of Warwick were reportedly being promoted and then taking place. The story of animal rights is synonymous with that of the birth and progression of the charity: Royal Society for the Prevention of Cruelty to Animals (RSPCA). The original Act of Parliament enacted during 1822, was known as 'Mr Martin's Bill', and became the precursor legislation associated with the formation of the Society for the Prevention of Cruelty to Animals (SPCA)[36]. His Bill gave some protection from abuse to domesticated animals such as cattle, but it had yet to include dogs.

On the 12th February 1824, Mr Richard Martin of Galway was given leave in the House of Commons to amend the original Bill of 1822 to give legal protection to other animals[37]. Under the heading 'Cruelty to Animals', Martin moved to increase the number of animals covered by the said Act to include dogs. His purpose, reports the *Morning Post*, was in fact 'to make mal-treatment of any animal a misdemeanour'. So began the long road to improving animal welfare in this country. On the same day, Martin proposed another Bill to cover the abolition of Bear baiting[38]. Up and down the country, Martin insisted, people were prepared to petition in favour of his Bills, but there was resistance in Parliament to having an additional Bill for Bear-baiting and other 'sports involving fighting animals. After consideration, Martin withdrew this Bill in favour of amending existing legislation at some time.

CRUELTY TO ANIMALS.

Mr. R. MARTIN, anticipating no objection to the motion which he had to make, would not trespass long on the attention of the House. The object which he had in view was to amend the Bill which he had formerly brought in, as certain animals had been omitted in it which were as well entitled to protection as others to which it extended He wished it to extend to dogs. An Hon. Friend near him wished to know if it would comprehend rats.—(*A laugh.*)—This was a subject on which he might touch at a future period. He, however, thought the proposed extension of the provisions of the Bill could not be objected to. He had read of an unfortunate dog, on whom a fishmonger had thrown scalding water, and injured the animal so that it came into the street and expired. In another instance oil of vitriol had been thrown on a creature of the same species. He hoped, without affecting more sensibility than others felt, he might be allowed to entertain a wish that a stop should be put to such barbarities. What reason was there why the animals he had mentioned should not be protected as others were? He should wish to make mal-treatment of any animal a misdemeanor. There was no reason why a man should not be tried at the Quarter Sessions for such an offence, though he by no means wished to take away the summary jurisdiction of the Magistrates.' For cruelty to horses in the streets it might be a sufficient punishment to inflict a fine of 5*l.*, or to commit the offender for three months. But there were some cruelties, such as a late case, where a parcel of horses had been burned to death, which he most potently believed would not be adequately visited by either of the inflictions he had mentioned. In the town of Holywell a wretch had fixed a horse over a slow fire, and kept the animal in that situation till the whole contents of the abdomen had tumbled out. No man could say that the Magistrates possessed the means of adequately punishing such enormities. He wished to correct this defect, and he had now stated the whole object of the Bill. He then moved for leave to bring in a Bill to amend the former Act.

Lord STANLEY seconded the motion.—Leave was given.

The Morning Post Feb 12 1824

Mr Martin, on behalf of a group of well-meaning and caring persons, was one of the first people to afford the idea that animals have rights and his first Bill stipulated that anyone ill-treating larger animals faced a fine of up to £5 or imprisonment for up to two months. Few Magistrates took much notice to this first animal rights law, thinking it to be a bit of a joke and that no one cared about the feelings of animals. Martin, being incredibly frustrated by such apathy, on one ocassion brought a poorly treated donkey into a court as evidence of cruelty and the somewhat shocked and faltering Magistrate eventually fined the owner, one Bill Burns for cruelty[39]. Mr Martin had received the publicity he sought for his law. On thw 16th June 1824, the Society for the Prevention of Cruelty to Animals (SPCA) was formed at Old Slaughter's Coffee House in St Martin's Lane, London.

At the very first meeting of the Society, the following minutes

were recorded (spelling as per the original document):

"At a meeting of the Society instituted for the purpose of preventing cruelty to animals, on the 16 th day of June 1824, at Old Slaughter's Coffee House, St. Martin's Lane: T F Buxton Esqr, MP, in the Chair,

It was resolved:

That a committee be appointed to superintend the Publication of Tracts, Sermons, and similar modes of influencing public opinion, to consist of the following Gentlemen:

Sir Jas. Mackintosh MP, A Warre Esqr. MP, Wm. Wilberforce Esqr. MP, Basil Montagu Esqr., Revd. A Broome, Revd. G Bonner, Revd G A Hatch, A E Kendal Esqr., Lewis Gompertz Esqr., Wm. Mudford Esqr., Dr. Henderson.

Resolved also:

That a Committee be appointed to adopt measures for Inspecting the Markets and Streets of the Metropolis, the Slaughter Houses, the conduct of Coachmen, etc.- etc, consisting of the following Gentlemen:

T F Buxton Esqr. MP, Richard Martin Esqr., MP, Sir James Graham, L B Allen Esqr., C C Wilson Esqr., Jno. Brogden Esqr., Alderman Brydges, A E Kendal Esqr., E Lodge Esqr., J Martin Esqr. T G Meymott Esqr.

A. Broome,

Honorary Secretary

The Mr Wheeler, whom Wombwell had denied that he had ever met at Warwick, had become the first inspector for the Society. Together with a second inspector, Mr Charles Teasdale, they immediately set about obtaining convictions against Smithfield Market and other meat traders. Some 63 defendants were successfully prosecuted for cruelty to animals in their care.

Financially though, the Society suffered greatly during its early days and Wheeler had to be dismissed due to a lack of funds. Mr Wheeler however, remained with the SPCA as a volunteer and it would probably have been in that capacity that his name became involved in the events at Warwick. What stands out from the many convictions he and his assistant Teasdale secured, is the location - Smithfield Market. This is of course the same location that hosted the annual Bartholomew Fair. Smithfield has been a centuries old location of repute in English social history. It was the site on which the Scotsman William Wallace was executed in 1305 and also where Wat Tyler, the English poll tax rioter was slain by Kingsmen during the Peasant's Revolt of 1381.

However, it had been primarily known as a marketplace for

meat for many centuries. The *Farmer's Magazine,* January –

June 1849 has a vivid description of the market during Victorian

times, as follows[40]

In 1848, however, we are not so squeamish. In the course of a year 220,000 head of cattle and 1,500,000 sheep are violently forced into an area of five acres, in the very heart of London, through its narrowest and most crowded thoroughfares; and are there sold, and there slaughtered, in the dark and undrained cellars, stables, and out-houses adjoining.

The inhabitants and shopkeepers, on the line of march taken by these herds and flocks, are weekly frighted from their propriety by the transit of 4,000 oxen and 30,000 sheep, that are hurried along by reckless drovers, and maddened by savage dogs. Scarcely a market-day

Excerpt from 'Smithfield Cattle Market',
The Farmer's Magazine, Volume 19, January – June, 1849, p. 142

passes without some grave accident to man, beast, and property. A letter from "An Inhabitant of West Smithfield," which will be found elsewhere in our columns, depicts, with the graphic force of truth, the grievous inconveniences and outrages to which those who reside in the neighbourhood of this intolerable nuisance are constantly subjected. The environs of Smithfield are poisoned by blood and garbage; the quality of the meat that we daily eat is deteriorated by the ill-usage which the animals undergo whilst alive, and by the faulty accommodation for cleansing and dressing it when dead. The graziers, who send their stock to London, are fleeced, in consequence of the monopoly which the Smithfield salesmen enjoy; and the poor of the metropolis are sickened by the pestilential trash which the crowded and undisciplined state of the meat markets enables the lower classes of salesmen to foist upon them with impunity. The cruelties, too, practised habitually on the wretched animals defy exaggeration. It will

Excerpt from 'Smithfield Cattle Market',
The Farmer's Magazine, Volume 19, January – June, 1849, p. 142

Describing the place, the author highlights the 'violence' of forcing large numbers of sheep and cattle into a five acre area, the narrator having reached this point via 'narrow thoroughfares'. It must have been a sight that even the least sensitive person today might not be able to have stood by and remain silent about the conditions in the market. It was an obvious place for the SPCA to start enforcing the recent Animal Rights legislation. The annual Bartholomew Fair could have only further antagonised the local population, which had consisted of not just tradesmen reliant on the market, but also consisted of bankers and solicitors amongst other professions. Members of these professions had lobbied Parliament to have the Smithfield 'nuisance' removed permanently as the *Farmer's Market* journal had explained[41].

Such is the law as declared by the greatest legal authorities of the land. Let us now see what is the view of the "merchant princes" and bankers of London. In Petitions to the Houses of Lords and Commons the following firms, among others, offer to advance their money to be heard by Counsel, Agents, &c., against the continuance of the Smithfield-market *nuisance*.

Barnett, Hoare, and Co.
Hanburys, Taylor, and Lloyd.
Cunliffes, Brooke, and Co.
Lubbock, Foster, and Co.
Smith, Payne, and Smiths.
Magniac, Jardine, and Co.
Roberts, Curtis, and Co.
Overend, Gurney, and Co.
Hankey and Co.
Jones Loyd and Co.
Baring Brothers.
Crawford, Colvin, and Co.
Johnson and Co.
William Tait.
Francis Ede and Son.
W. Bell and Co.
Ricketts, Boutcher, and Co.
Sanderson and Co.
F. A. Lizardi and Co.
Benjn. Elkin and Son.
Mangles and Co.
J. W. Welch.
Small and Co.
Robt. Eglinton and Co.
H. G. Abott.
John Gore and Co.
Roberts, Mitchell, and Co.
Rawson, Norton, and Co.
Daniell, Dickenson, and Co.
Enthoven and Co.

Melville and Co.
W. Anderson, sen., and Co.
James Alexander.
Jamieson, Brothers, and Co.
Geo. Little and Co.
Josh. Templeman and Co.
Siordet, Meyer, and Co.
Emanuel, Henry, and Co.
Emanuel Henry Brandth.
Lyall, Brothers, and Co.
Burmeston Brothers.
Thos. Stephens and Co.
Albert Pelly and Co.
Gonne, Lucas, and Gribble.
Sinclair, Hamilton, and Co.
Jno. H. Rudall.
Gillespies, Moffatt, and Co.
A. Stewart and Westmoreland
Lesley Alexander and Co.
J. S. Neave.
John Entwisle.
Kelsall and Co.
M. Hetherington and Co.
Barclay, Brothers, and Co.
Gregson and Co.
Drewett and Fowler.
Prescott, Grote, and Co.
H. J. Johnston and Co.
Barnard and Co.
Williams, Deacon, and Co.

Excerpt from 'Smithfield Cattle Market',

The Farmer's Magazine, Volume 19, January – June, 1849, p. 142

Laton, Hulbert, and Co.	John Feltham and Co.
John Allen and Co.	A. Macdonald and Co.
Hibbert and Co.	G. C. Jackson and Co.
Davidsons and Co.	Trumpter and Rouquette.
John Locke and Co.	Boyon, Hoyer, and Tagart.
Gonger and Steuart.	W. W. Forbes.
Warre Brothers.	Charles Ball and Co.
Moffatt and Co.	Gibson, Linton, and Co.
Innes, Hodge, and Co.	F. and A. Bovet.
J. Mallett.	W. Markland.
W. Moberley, Son, and Co.	Quarles Harris and Sons.
Alexander Cullen and Co.	Collmann and Stolterfoht.
Alison, Cumberlege, and Co.	Jos. Edermann.
Geo. Pye and Co.	Peter Dickson and Co.
G. W. Harrison.	Newman, Hunt, and Co.
Gledstones and Co.	Boyds and Thomas.
T. Green and Co.	Williams and Co.
Dickson Brothers.	Harvey, Brand, and Co.
Bensler, James, and Co.	Anderson, Brothers, and Co.
Donaldson, Lambert, and Co.	Sohn. Hart and Co.
Wood, Brothers, and Co.	Martin, Stones, and Co.
F. Le Breton.	Brown, Janson, and Co.
Blyth and Greene.	Spooner, Attwood, and Co.
John Routh.	Saunderson, Fry, and Fry.
Dallas and Coles.	

Excerpt from 'Smithfield Cattle Market',

The Farmer's Magazine, Volume 19, January – June, 1849, p. 142

Despite the impressive list of support for banning Smithfield's operation, this weighty body of City based bankers and professionals could still not prevent the market from continuing its trade, which it carries on till this day, albeit in a more orderly, highly regulated manner with no live animals in sight.

Animal welfare had not escaped William Hone's printing press either. The *Every-Day Book* published a letter from one 'J.B.' on the subject of cruelty to animals and the prevention thereof. 'The inhuman rate at which horses are driven in stage coaches, conduces greatly to mortality; this consumption of animal life is, in some instances, one in three annually', writes the author. Hone published this in the book on the page for June 16[th][42].

Hone is therefore not averse to publicising the subject of cruelty to animals. Conversely, in 1830, Hone printed a new edition of the popular *The Sports and Pastimes of the People of England* by Joseph Strutt. In this new edition, Hone had produced a copious index to Strutt's original text, the original being full of articles concerning fox hunting as well as several on the so-called sport of bear and other animal baiting. Strutt writes, 'the following pastimes he [Englishman] considers as common both in town and country, namely, 'bull-baitings and bear-baitings, in which our countrymen and citizens greatly delight, and frequently use'[43]. But Strutt's text is directed to earlier centuries and in particular the Elizabethan era. In the 19th century and up to the 1835 Cruelty to Animals Act, this so-called bull-baiting still attracted some following[44]. One report from the 1849 indicated that bull-rings were still to be seen in some towns. 'At Grantham' for instance, 'we believe, the ring at which the tortured bull was pinned by the nose, and there baited by bull-dogs, is still to be seen'[45]. Even today the centre of Birmingham has its Bull-Ring albeit now a name for a shopping centre!

A newspaper report during 1825 announced the following[46]:

> Through the efforts of the Society for the Prevention of Cruelty to Animals, 144 convictions for cruel treatment of animals have taken place in the past year, chiefly among bullock-drovers; but partly also among those who have the care of horses. The Report of the Society states that there is ground to hope for an entire abolition of bull-baiting, at no distant period. throughout the country: bear-baiting, badger-baiting, and cock-fighting, are also becoming daily less frequent.

The Bury and Norwich Post (Bury Saint Edmunds, England),

Wednesday, September 07, 1825; Issue 2254

However, the practice of bear-baiting had still not completely been eradicated. Even in the centre of London bear-baiting was carried out. A report from a concerned spectator was published about the sport in Holborn, London. Reading this vivid description from *The Standard*, during 1828, it is clear that public opinion was turning against such sports and patience had finally become exhausted[47].

DOG FIGHTING AND BEAR BAITING,
GREEN DRAGON-YARD, HOLBORN.

This pit, as it is called, is a loft about 25 feet square, with a fire-place, and in one corner of the apartment is a space enclosed with green baize, where the proprietor, his wife, and children sleep and eat. Two bears, several dogs, foxes, and badgers, are chained to the wall all around, many of which are in cages heaped upon each other.

The centre is enclosed with boards about three feet high, containing an area of about eight feet square, where the dogs fight, and bears and badgers are baited. On entering this elegant amphitheatre, the smell, as may be well supposed, is most offensive, and the noise of dogs, bears, and rabble most appalling, and forming a nuisance to the whole neighbourhood.

The company consist of butchers, brickmakers, and others, who do not appear to live by honest industry. These are the fellows who mostly bring the dogs. About an hour and a half is spent in dog-fighting ; then the bear is brought forward, and fastened to a ring in the centre of the pit, with a chain about two feet in length, when one dog at a time is slipped at him.

The whole concludes with a badger-bait. The animal is confined in a long cage, and a door at one end being opened, as with the bear one dog at a time is slipped. In one case, the bear being very young was much lacerated by several fierce bull-dogs, and bled profusely, but still evinced, though unmuzzled, the utmost docility and good-nature, holding up his bleeding paw as if to reproach his cruel master. He was led in and out by a little boy, who, in the intervals of torture, rode on his back.

The greatest cruelty occurs when what are called matches take place, the dogs frequently fighting till one or both are killed.   A SPECTATOR.

The Standard (London, England), Friday, July 11, 1828; Issue 359

The practice had become rarer, although several newspaper reports did appear after 1830. This one, from a Sheffield newspaper, might otherwise be considered amusing if it was not for the cruelty that must have occurred. The report also hints at Royal approval for the distasteful pastime[48].

CAUTION TO THE ITINERANTS.— *Thomas Shirt*, an aged man shaking with the palsy, was brought up by the constables of Bradfield, and charged with publicly baiting a bear, to the breach of the King's peace. In reply to this charge, the old man said, that "he had had but two or three slips we't." and that he had his Majesty's authority to bait his animal when and where he thought proper. In proof of this authority, the defendant produced a tin case, from which he took a sheet of parchment, printed and written upon, purporting to be a license issued from the Lord Chamberlain's Office, and signed by Thomas Lister Parker, Esq.. sergeant trumpeter, authorising him, in consideration of the sum of two pounds. to play a drum, and sound a trumpet, at and in all times and places to him convenient. The magistrate explained to the old man, that his "trumpet license" gave him no authority "to play" his bear, and that the baiting of that or any other animal was a brutal amusement, which the magistrates would not permit. The poor fellow was permitted to depart without charges.

The Sheffield Independent, and Yorkshire and Derbyshire Advertiser (Sheffield, England),

Saturday, May 28, 1831; Issue 597

Clearly the defendant was trying to pull a fast one or maybe was illiterate and had wasted his £2 on a worthless license. Even later than 1835, several reports of bear-baiting appeared in the newspapers. The authorities commented via a brief item in many newspapers, this one being the *Leicester Chronicle* of 1837

PROTECTION OF ANIMALS FROM CRUELTY.—We believe it
is very little known, that by a late Act of Parliament, relative to cruelty to animals, dog-fighting as well as cock-
fighting is prohibited. Bull-baiting, bear-baiting, and the
like, are also embraced in this humane statute.

The Leicester Chronicle (Leicester, England),

Saturday, August 05, 1837; pg. [1]; Issue 1394

It was a reminder that bear and other animal baiting had already

been outlawed[49]. The 1835 Act amended the existing legislation

to include (as 'cattle') bulls, dogs, bears, goats and sheep, and to

prohibit bating of such[50].

We have seen that since the first parliamentary airing in 1822,

laws pertaining to animal welfare had progressed through the

next two decades into an increasingly effective legal protection

for mainly domestic animals. The development of a national

society (eventually the RSPCA), had developed a partially

effective legal inspectorate which had begun to bear fruit in the

courts with multiple convictions of animal cruelty. Apart from

Bears and Bulls, protection of cruelty to wild beats was still not within the framework of such laws. Nevertheless, the inspectorate took it on themselves to comment, through the newspapers, about the events in Warwick.

Wild beasts had been considered for protection by law as early as 1819[51]. During a speech to Parliament on considering 'the law as it respected wild animals reclaimed from their original barbarism and natural ferocity', Mr Marmaduke Lawson (MP for Boroughbridge), claimed the law was defective in this respect. 'Whenever any animal of whatever description, became of delight or use to its master, his law should protect it', he stated. He then proceeded to reason why menageries should be included within a legal framework.

> 'For what just reason could be assigned for not protecting the property of Mr. Polito, or any other proprietor of wild beasts who resided in town, or who travelled through the country? Such animals ought, indeed, upon every just ground, to be protected by law; for their general exhibition was known to be of great utility, especially to the youth of both sexes, in presenting them with a practical illustration of the natural history of those animals.'

There was no mention of cruelty though, Lawson's objective was to create a law that would protect them from such things as theft. The basis for this was that they were the property of their owners and should be treated in a similar manner to those of domestic animals. As a deterrent and in the event of a court decision, Lawson proposed transportation or whipping for the guilty defendant. Finally, he asked that 'leave be given to bring in a Bill to amend the laws for the protection of Wild Animals reclaimed and retained as private property'. On Division, the motion was defeated, even after having gained the support of the Attorney General.

Whoever it was that compiled the newspaper report of the events at Warwick for The *Liverpool Mercury* on Friday, July 29, 1825 , in which they claimed that according to the Attorney General, 'anyone wantonly maiming any animal, either by setting dogs at it or otherwise, is liable to transportation', must first surely have consulted the law before making such a claim[52].

It is though incorrect at the date of publication of the report,

since wild beasts were still not protected by the first of the

Animal Cruelty Acts. If anything, it provides further suspicion

as to the validity of *The Liverpool Mercury* report and the

numerous other newspaper reports during the July and August of

1825, all describing in some detail, one or even two fights

arranged by Wombwell between lions and dogs at Warwick.

Earlier Reports of Animal Fights and Newspaper articles.

There can be no firm conclusions from the above evidence that the Warwick events either did or did not take place, although some doubts have now emerged as to the validity of newspaper reports. Evidence is required from other sources of information of the period, in an effort to be sure either way. But, other evidence is not forthcoming from sources outside of the newspapers and journals of the time. It is therefore necessary to look at more newspaper reports, but this time at those that appeared before the alleged events at Warwick had taken place.

The first ever newspaper report hinting that a lion and dog fight had been rumoured appears to be during April 1825, some three months prior to the widely reported event, when the *Hampshire Telegraph and Sussex Chronicle*, amongst others no doubt, reports that 'the account of a match being made between Wombwell's Lion Nero and six mastiffs, at Warwick, proves a hoax'[53]. This succinct statement appears in the *RACING* column of that newspaper, so I suggest that the original rumour may

have been a verbal one and that some racing correspondent had

picked up on it very early in its manifestation. That report was

on the 11th of April 1825, but even before that the well-

established *Morning Chronicle* on the morning of 4th April

1825, published under the title 'The Lion Fight – A Hoax', an

article on the affair thus:

'A most impudent *hoax* has recently been practicing on
the public, through the medium of County Journals, to
which we have unintentionally given currency. We allude
to the announcement of an intended fight between a lion
belonging to Mr. Wombwell, an itinerant showman, and
six British mastiffs, on Worcester racecourse. The object
of putting forth such a report is manifest; it would of
course excite curiosity, and induce persons to flock to see
the lion which was about to be engaged in so serious a
contest. We have made enquiries as to the probability of
the story, and find it to be altogether undeserving of
credit, and to be just as probable as the old humbug of
the fight with the Norwich Bull, of which Mr. Wombwell
was also the parent. In order to carry on the joke, it was
stated last week, in a provincial paper, that a temporary
Amphitheatre was to be erected on Worcester racecourse,
with a den in the centre, 36 feet in circumference, and it
was added, that the lion was four feet and a half in
height, and thirteen feet in length. A moment's reflection
ought to convince any person that this must be false,
inasmuch as there never was a lion in existence of such
magnitude, thirteen feet being about the length of two

prize oxen together, and completely out of proportion with the alleged height. But Mr. Wombwell's is not the only ingenious speculation on public credibility, for we yesterday saw, in a Morning paper, an account of a lion fight with six dogs, which was stated to have actually taken place on Tuesday last, for 5,000 sovereigns, on Warwick race course, in which a circumstantial account of the battle is given, with the names of the dogs, and the men by whom they were handled, together with a triumphant description of Nero, the lion's victory over his canine assailants. This all looked very plausible, and we were almost duped into belief of its truth; but, before we adopted the account, we proceeded to Mr. Cross's, at Exeter 'Change and made enquiries, when our eyes were at once opened. A bill was placed in our hands, issued by Earl James and Sons – the proprietors of the notorious *Bonassus* – in which we found an account, word for word, similar to that published yesterday, of a fight between same lion, and the same six dogs, alleged to have taken place for 600 sovereigns in Lancashire, on the 14th of January 1824. The one story turns out to be just as worthy of credit as the other; and if confirmation be wanted, on referring to the Warwick and Birmingham Papers of this week, the subject is not even alluded to. Had the fight taken place, these Journals would scarcely be silent on so interesting an occurrence – From *Bell's Life in London*[54].

Not only had the idea been dismissed as a hoax, it seems that the reports from July 1825 had actually been copied, word for word, from these earlier reports during April 1825. Credit must go to *The Morning Chronicle* staff for checking with the famous 'Cross's Menagerie' along the Strand in central London[55]. Here, one Earl James (Earl James & Sons), another popular menagerist, had been credited with the report of a similar match as in Warwick, this time in Lancashire during 1824. This match attracted a prize of 600 Sovereigns to the winner. Earl James' establishment also billed a weird beast under the name of *Bonassus*, 'having the head of an Elephant, the forepart of a Bison, the mane of a Lion, the eye on the cheek and an ear similar to a human being'[56]. A handbill James created, advertised and emphasised the strange nature of this beast, but it turned out to be an American Bison, which had not been seen in the UK until then.

During April and May 1821, Earl James (billed as J.E. James) advertised his thanks for Royal and popular patronage at his menagerie at 287, Strand, London during the previous six months and promised the following exhibition:

> 'The BONASSUS, from the Appalachian Mountains of America, is seventeen months old, five feet ten inches high, and is particularly interesting to the Naturalist, Man of Science, Philosopher and Historian; and has recently excited the unqualified admiration of his Royal Highness, the Duke of Gloucester, Duchesses of Clarence and Kent, Princess Feodore and Prince Ernest, who with a numerous retinue, honoured the Exhibition with their presence.[57]'

He continues to list Royal and establishment patronage to include the Bishops of London, Carlisle and Oxford as having already visited the exhibition together with 'Officers of his Majesty's Naval and Military Service.' All these people, claims James, have witnessed 'the Exhibition of the Greatest Wonder in Natural History that ever crossed the Atlantic Ocean.' With an admittance at 1 shilling it was not though, a cheap day out for London's poor.

On Wednesday 13th June 1821, James advertised again. This time it was to announce the attendance of 'His Grace the Duke of Wellington' who had commented that 'neither in Europe or India had he ever seen or heard of such an extraordinary animal.[58]'

This type of publication, Helen Cowie explains in her accompanying text to the handbill, has two effects[59]. Firstly, to advertise the overall size and physical description of such beasts, their rarity and other attributes. Secondly, and perhaps more importantly, to provide the reader with an 'overall visitor experience'. Thus, it is not surprising to find examples such as the *Bonassus* promising a new experience and descriptions like 'huge and terrific' to get audiences to pay for entry to the menagerie with the promise of a glimpse of such beasts.

It is the Exeter 'Change handbill that is most interesting. It suggests that unnamed menagerists were using paper communications to pre-announce a lion and dog fight well before the events at Warwick were being reported. Therefore, it is highly likely that a handbill or maybe even a succession of handbills existed well before 1825 advertising similar forthcoming events. I have previously reported the existence of handbills that report escaped beasts only to find they invariably happen at fictitious towns or on roads to and from places far too far apart to be a credible journey[60]. It is increasingly likely therefore, that the events at Warwick never actually took place and that an elaborate hoax by some person or persons perpetuated the rumours that had surfaced via, in the first place, *Bell's Life in London* (see below) and then faithfully reproduced by *the Morning Chronicle* during the early months of 1825[61].

One of the newspapers that had also carried early rumours of the fight was the *Caledonian Mercury (Edinburgh, Scotland)*. On Thursday, February 24, 1825, it carried a small insert under another concerning the bare knuckle fighter Jem Ward, being now prepared to fight Tom Cannon[62] [63]. This was several weeks before either the *Hampshire Telegraph* or *Morning Chronicle* reports and is likely to be the first written appearance

concerning any lion fighting with dogs arranged by a named

menagerist. It reads:

> 'The fight between Mr Wombwell's lion, Nero, lately
> exhibited in the north, and six English mastiffs, or bull
> dogs, is finally determined upon, and the scene of action
> will take place at either Worcester or Warwick. Betting is
> in favour of Nero.'

Clearly there was confusion over the location of the proposed

contest, but both Warwick and Worcester were race courses and

both popular with a growing audience of gamblers. It was both

Worcester and Warwick that were mentioned in the handbill,

according to *Bell's Life in London* report. The Jem Ward/Tom

Cannon was still not billed at this stage, but would, in any event,

take place at Warwick, according to later reports, on the 19th

July 1825. There seems to a concerted effort on behalf of editors

to conflate the knuckle fights with those between lions and dogs.

In June of the same year, again before the fight was supposed to

take place, the prestigious *London Times* carried a report (which

it claimed to be from the Shrewsbury Chronicle) consisting of the following statement:

> THE LION NERO AND THE DOGS. - [from the
> Shrewsbury Chronicle] - "Whatever may be the
> result of the preparation for this mortal combat, it
> is certain that the field of battle is now already
> provided. Mr Wombwell on Monday last
> inspected the cage or den (which has been built
> by Messrs. Drayton and Rowlands in this town),
> and, expressed great confidence of retaining, not
> only his 5000 guineas, but the lordly brute on
> whose head they are staked. The den is 57 feet in
> circumference, 15 feet high, formed of strong iron
> bars seven or eight inches distant from each other,
> and covered in with a wooden roof, removable at
> pleasure with its boarded floor. The whole will be
> fixed upon axle-trees and wheels. Mr Wombwell
> will not say when the battle is to take place. A
> gentleman of Shrewsbury has offered to secure
> him 1000l [pounds] if he would fight it in this
> neighbourhood: this, at present, is refused. – The
> prices to see the battle will be as follows: - Boxes
> 3l 3s., Pit 2l 2s.,
> Gallery 1 1s.[64]

This report appears to promote the town of Shrewsbury as being

integral to the forthcoming fight.

The firm of 'Messrs. Drayton and Rowlands' would, apparently,

be building the den and a 'gentleman of Shrewsbury' had

offered Wombwell a large reward for the fight to take place in

the town. There was however, no firm under that name in the

town, according to local trade directories of the period. The

sheer size of the construction indicated a dimension of 57 feet

across and the movement of such a structure from Shrewsbury

to Warwick (or even Worcester) would entail planning and

logistics comparable to those moving similarly large structures

in the present day. The report is pure fantasy, made up of

hearsay from elsewhere and some enterprising conjecture,

probably conjured up by the reporter or one of his associates, to

promote the town. However, the *Times* newspaper was

impressed enough to also republish it.

> The account of a match being made between Wombwell's Lion Nero and six mastiffs, at Warwick, proves a hoax.

Hampshire Telegraph and Sussex Chronicle etc (Portsmouth, England), Monday,
April 11, 1825; Issue 1331

The above small insert was placed in the *Hampshire Telegraph*

and Sussex Chronicle during April 1825, showing that fervour surrounding the forthcoming event was obviously now on the

wane and it was being considered an anti-climax[65]. This item

was published on the 11th April and I can only presume they had

been informed by the *Morning Chronicle* article of the 4th of

April 1825, unequivocally denouncing the fight as a complete

hoax and, reading between the lines, also condemning the

provincial journals for bringing it to their attention. One such

provincial newspaper had inserted a correction after reading the

'Hoax' report from a national newspaper[66].

101

Excerpt from *Berrow's Worcester Journal (Worcester, England)*, Thursday, April 07, 1825; Issue 6379

This did not stop *Berrow's Worcester Journal*, announcing to the people of the town that:

'Mr Wombwell advertises that the grand combat between Nero, the great lion, and the dogs, will positively take place at Warwick, on the 26th of July; the ground appointed is surrounded with high walls, on which seats will be erected. – The Den has been removed from Shrewsbury to Northampton'[67].

This statement, placed on the 7th of April, must have added to the confusion and implies that Wombwell was maybe at the heart of this hoax after all. On May 19th 1825 the same publication announces that Wombwell was now considering a venue 'at some place within 100 miles of London'[68].

Wombwell seemed never to let a good opportunity pass him by to get people to his Menagerie. It is perfectly possible that he advertised an event building up to one that would take place in Warwick, but not before also announcing on several occasions that it would be at Worcester or 'somewhere within 100 miles of London' leaving the public somewhat confused as to the whereabouts of the actual lion fight.

Bell's Life in London, a then recently created weekly, had warned George Wombwell of the consequences of such a match between a lion and six dogs as early as 6th March 1825. They had warned him 'not to attempt the *wolf* and the *crane*'[69]. Alluding to the fable attributed to Aesop, the periodical suggested that even though the crane possessed good luck and managed to draw his head out of the wolf's mouth unhurt, that it did not follow that 'Mr W. is to draw his head in safety out of the lion's den'[70]. It may just be that the passions of men and women might be so aroused, 'like a lion [...] once aroused', that one should guard against the consequences of such anger as may happen following such a match.

This thinly veiled threat to Wombwell as to the likely consequences, and was probably the first published sign of a spirited conspiracy by the establishment, which would include both men and women, even though the latter would be a 'rare' intervention. So we may surmise that as early as March 1825, some influential persons were admitting to the possibility of an intervention to prevent the events at Warwick whenever they might happen. 'Gratitude and Greed Go Not Together', as Aesop's wolf had implied to the lucky crane after extracting his head from the wolf's mouth!

By 3rd April 1825, *Bell's Life in London* had published their own

'Hoax' article under the title 'The Lion Fight – Fudge!'[71]. This

article was republished by *The Morning Chronicle* a day later as

previously indicated (see earlier). Not to be outdone by all the

publicity afforded the fight, *Bell's Life in London* published

Wombwell's letter from Loughborough dated 13th April 1825.

> **THE CHALLENGE TO NERO.**
> **TO THE EDITOR OF BELL'S LIFE IN LONDON.**
> Sir,—In your Paper of the 10th inst. it is stated, that, by an application to you, my lion may be matched with six dogs, for the sum of 200 sovereigns. In answer to which I have to state, that Nero has long been matched. Was he not, so paltry a sum as 200 would not induce me to bring him forward; but, as I am willing to oblige all parties, I have a very fine lion, cubbed in Scotland, and called Wallace, now five years old, as fine a lion as any in England, excepting Nero, which I shall have no objection of matching against the six dogs in question, for the aforesaid sum of two hundred, provided the person who finds the dogs is at the expence of erecting a building sufficient for the combat, and they may appoint their own place and time. Any intimation from the parties, inserted in your Paper, I will reply to.—I am, Sir, your's, most respectfully,
> GEO. WOMBWELL.
>
> Royal Menagerie, Loughbro'. 13th April, 1825.

Bells Life in London and Sporting Chronicle, Sunday 17 April 1825

This letter appeared in response to a challenge set out by *Bell's*

Life in London on the 10th of the month thus:

> 'The Lion Nero – We have received a letter from Mr
> Wombwell, dated Newcastle under Lyme, Staffordshire,
> in which he gives us his '*word*' that the combat between
> the lion and the dogs, is bound to take place, and that the
> cage is now preparing by Messrs. Drayton and Co.,
> smiths and wheelwrights, Welsh Bridge, Shrewsbury.
> Next August, he says, is the time fixed – 'Seeing is
> believing,' they say.
> The Challenge to Nero – If Mr. Wombwell is serious in
> his proposal, to match the Lion against six English dogs,
> we are authorised to say, that the six dogs can be
> matched against him for Two Hundred Sovereigns,
> without delay. A note to us on the subject will be
> attended to. As for Mr. James's *a-la-mode-beef* Lion, one
> dog can be found to give him a *belly full*. Let Mr. James
> set his lion's back straight before he talks of fighting
> him. Mr Cross's lion in Exeter 'Change, is considerably
> larger than Nero[72].

Clearly, the periodical was referring to their article of the 3rd of

April 1825, then republished in *The Morning Chronicle* on the

4th April, and Wombwell had apparently reacted to both its

publication and the 'Challenge' set out by *Bell's Life in London*

on the 3rd of the month. Wombwell's letter suggests a match

between the dogs and his five-year-old lion, Wallace. However,

the fact he challenges whosoever is willing to let six dogs go

into a lion's den, with the task of building a suitable place for the combat and to erect a building for the fight to take place, suggests to me that it was never his intention to contest either of his lions with dogs anywhere in the country. It also points to Wombwell not being the source of the original offers earlier in the year for fights at either Worcester or Warwick. Even so, Wombwell once again shows his enterprise in continuing the debate for publicity purposes.

Bell's Life in London once again entered the fray on 15th May 1825, with an announcement that the 'den intended for the approaching combat is now complete' and that those wishing to reserve tickets should 'send their names to the Offices of *Bell's,* or *Egan's Life in London* newspapers'[73].

This announcement finished with the line - 'Royal Menagerie, Coventry 11th May' so it may be another advert for the contest placed by Wombwell himself as a promotion for his regular travelling menagerie or possibly one made up by *Bell's* to keep the interest going. There's every chance that attendances at Wombwell's menagerie were on the rise, given the publicity it was receiving during March and April that year. By July 31st 1825, the *Bell's* periodical was reporting that the fight, long thought to be a 'hoax', had in fact taken place, which was then followed by a detailed account as were the reports making the rounds in the local newspapers, word for word. *Bell's* was not to be outdone by their competitors around the country! After all, selling newspapers was their business.

In the very same edition in July, on page 248, *Bell's* carried a description of the meeting by Wheeler, the agent for the Society for the Prevention of Cruelty to Animals, with the Lord Mayor of London which was called with the aim of getting Wombwell banned from Bartholomew Fair[74]. It was again word for word with those entries in some national and local papers already mentioned above. The juxtaposition of a report of the lion fight at Warwick with the report of the meeting with the Lord Mayor are quite revealing in that they repeat verbatim published reports from other newspapers. *Bell's Life in London* was now no different in their handling of the events at Warwick than the other national and local papers. There were though, no mention of their efforts to secure a place for the events to take place nor their offer of a prize. If they had been behind the events, they would surely have wanted their newspaper to have advertised their involvement. It could be that with all the bad publicity across the country they decided to play down any efforts they made or more likely, their previous offers were as fictitious as was the match between lions and dogs in the first place.

Bell's periodical, on the 7th August 1825 became further entangled in the events by publishing this lengthy description of the events at Warwick together with the alleged letter from Wombwell at Alcester concerning the condition of his lion, Nero, the day after the alleged fight[75]. More interesting was the very next letter to the editor. It was published under the title 'Audi alteram partam'[76]:

109

"Audi alteram partem."

TO THE EDITOR OF BELL'S LIFE IN LONDON.

Sir,—A constant reader of your Journal entreats publication to the following observations :—From the space you devoted last week to a description of that most cruel and soul-harrowing exhibition, the lion and dog fight at Warwick, I should hope you would not discard the short and undigested remarks of an advocate to humanity, who blushed for the honour of England, while perusing a narrative so replete with circumstances of horror. And is it possible that in a nation denominated religious, civilized, moral, well-regulated, that there can be found a body of men willing to pay guineas and half-guineas for seats to witness a spectacle of brutal and determined ferocity—a contest unnatural in itself, from the wide dissimilarity between the victims of contention, and rendered a thousand times more so from the inhuman fact that the gentle, generous, and magnanimous Nero had lost the characteristics of a lion by the peculiar mode of bringing him up. Was it necessary to deprive him of his native energy, to rob him of that terrible magnificence the lion is invested with when as the King of the Forest he keeps all others in subjection,—was it necessary to tame, to domesticate, to convert his whole system into docility and gentleness, and then, regardless of his fidelity and affection, to expose him to the fury of six of the canine species, trained for fighting?—could any thing but the most mercenary spirit have dictated such barbarity?—could any breast, ever alive to the impressions of human sensibity, have resisted the mild and sensible exhortations of the amiable Quaker, whose act of humanity adds another striking feature to their many and correspondent virtues? O, Mr. Editor, I am sorry to say that the love of gain is a counterpoise for the refinements of the heart, that it is a succedaneum for common sense and right feeling ; but ill-gotten wealth never prospers. The wages of sin is death, and the triumphs of infamy are short and inglorious. The cruelty of this deed was likewise heightened by its taking place in a den, where the poor animals had not proper space for defence, a due advantage was not consequently given. I would further ask you, Sir, whether we are taking pattern by the example of the Romans, who exhibited in their colossal Amphitheatre, constructed for the purposes of hunting a combination of furious creatures, whose natures were as distinct and even more opposite than the lion and the dog : since tigers and the spotted hyena were contrasted with zebras and camel-leopards, who are, without exception, the most harmless animals of the forest. Such an indiscriminate massacre we are told afforded sport to ancient Rome; but little did I suppose it would be patronized by modern England. For Heaven's sake, Mr. Editor, if you can put a word towards excluding Mr. Wombwell from a seat in Bartholomew Fair, lose not the opportunity. A British public must revolt from his proceedings at Warwick, and a British public ought to evince its displeasure by withdrawing their countenance. Sir, I request at least that my sentiments, as an individual, may be promulgated through the medium of your columns.—I remain, Sir, the friend of humanity,

PHILOCOSMOS.

This, an anonymous letter to the editor on the events at Warwick, seemingly outraged the writer when hearing of such acts of 'barbarity'. They also liken the event to those of the Roman past and asks how could such an 'indiscriminate massacre [...] be patronized by modern England'. In the end, it seems obvious it was a thinly veiled threat to get George Wombwell banned from the Bartholomew Fair, and if not direct from the hand of a representative of the Society for the Prevention of Cruelty to Animals, it does resonate with the notions already alluded to, by their former inspector, Mr Wheeler. Thus, *Bell's* becomes once again sided with decency, despite their penchant for all things gambling and sporting activities such as knuckle fighting, badger baiting and dog fighting. After all, excitement and spectacle is what really sells the periodical.

The final report that is worth mentioning is the same as the 'HOAX' report mentioned earlier, but in this case it is the wording concerning a description of the event at Warwick, **three**

111

whole months before the event allegedly took place!

THE LION FIGHT.—A most impudent hoax has recently been practising on the public, through the medium of country journals. We allude to the announcement of an intended fight between a lion belonging to Mr.Wombwell, an itinerant showman, and six British mastiffs, on Worcester race-course. The object of putting forth such a report is manifest; it would of course excite curiosity, and induce persons to flock to see the lion which was about to be engaged in so serious a contest. In order to carry on the joke, it was stated last week, in a provincial paper, that a temporary amphitheatre was to be erected on Worcester race-course, with a den in the centre, 36 feet in circumference, and it was added, that the lion was four feet and a half in height, and thirteen feet in length. A moment's reflection ought to convince any person that this must be false, inasmuch as there never was a lion in existence of such magnitude, thirteen feet being about the length of two prize oxen together, and completely out of proportion with the alleged height. But Mr. Wombwell's is not the only ingenious speculation on public credulity, for we saw, in a Morning Paper, an account of a lion fight with six dogs, which was stated to have actually taken place on Tuesday last, for 5000 sovereigns, on Warwick race-course, in which a circumstantial account of the battle is given, with the names of the dogs, and the men by whom they were handled, together with a description of Nero, and his victory over his canine assailants. This all looked very plausible, and we were almost duped into a belief of its truth ; but, before we adopted the account, we proceeded to Mr. Cross's, at Exeter 'Change, and made inquiries. A bill was placed in our hands, issued by Earl James and Sons—the proprietors of the notorious Bonassus ; in which we found an account, word for word, similar to that published, of a fight between the same lion, and the same six dogs, alleged to have taken place for 600 sovereigns in Lancashire, on the 14th of January, 1824. The one story turns out to be just as worthy of credit as the other ; and if confirmation be wanted, on referring to the Warwick and Birmingham Papers of this week, the subject is not even alluded to.—*Morning Herald.*

Berkshire Chronicle - Saturday 09 April 1825

Note that the date of *The Berkshire Chronicle* is Saturday 9th

April, 1825, which had, according to the report, republished an

'account of a lion fight with six dogs' that had taken place on

Tuesday last' [which would have been 5th April], but that it had

been a hoax[77]. It states that the report was from the *Morning*

Herald which must have already published the account. It

mentions the six dogs, Warwick racecourse, 5000 guineas and

even the outcome of the event. This last piece of evidence is

more than convincing that the alleged events at Warwick simply

had not taken place either before 9th April 1825, as suggested by

the *Morning Herald* nor during the month of July that year as

suggested by many newspapers and periodicals across the

country.

If even more evidence is required that the later 1825 reports

were copied verbatim, was given in a newspaper article dated 7th

April 1825 in the *Worcester Journal*[78]. In this it describes how

the lion did not attempt to fight the dogs, the story of Mr

Wheeler going to Warwick and many other aspects of the event that were published up and down the country during the July and August of 1825. The 'Hoax' appears to have been carried out on the whole population and extended to both sides of the newspaper industry: editors *and* their readership.

The Lion Fight at Warwick.—By the details of this brutal exhibition which have been published, it appears that the Lion offered scarcely any resistance; having been in a state of confinement from his birth, and consequently unused to contend with other animals, he did not attempt to *fight* the dogs; when they fastened upon him, he shook them off; when they again seized his throat and head, he roared dreadfully, but evidently only from the pain he suffered—not from anger. As the dogs hung to his throat and head, he pawed them off by sheer strength, and in doing this, and rolling upon them, did them considerable mischief; but it amounts to a remarkable fact, that he never once *bit*, or attempted to bite, during the whole contest, nor seemed to desire to retaliate any of the punishment which was inflicted upon him by his trained and furious assailants; one of the dogs died in consequence of the injury he sustained.—It affords us great satisfaction to say that not only was Wombwell disappointed in the attendance of spectators, but his conduct in exposing the noble beast to be thus worried, has excited deep and general disgust; this feeling was very manifest among the most respectable inhabitants of Warwick. Mr. Wheeler, the Inspector to the Society for suppressing Cruelty to Animals, arrived there on Sunday; and on Monday, made application to the Mayor (Mr. Wilmhurst) to prevent the Lion Fight taking place; but the Magistrates refused his application, upon the ground that they could not *prevent* such an exhibition. Mr. Wheeler has stated that he had every reason to believe that the report that the fight was the consequence of a wager was utterly groundless, and that it was merely circulated to excite curiosity, congregate spectators, and make the lion produce more money.—On the day of the fight, a highly-respectable member of the Society of Friends, delivered the following letter to Wombwell, which was written by a *Friend*: this humane (though of course fruitless) endeavour to prevent the disgraceful scene, does the highest credit to the heart and feelings of the writer:—

Understanding the Events in a Wider Context

With a detailed consideration of the events at Warwick, we begin to build a picture of George's life, not least through the criticism of contemporary protagonists that involved themselves with the lion and dog fights and with the politics of the continuation of Bartholomew Fair in London. How then do we make assertions, from what we now know as the mythical 'events', and how do they inform us about George Wombwell the person, his position in late Georgian society and how do we account for the previously unflinching devotion to a single characterisation, based on Warwick, that has remained firm in most writer's minds for almost two centuries?

If one reviews some established texts concerning the events at Warwick, one finds that every single one has accepted that the lion fights actually took place. Even in later texts such as Helen Cowie's *Exhibiting Animals in Nineteenth Century Britain* (2014), the author devotes several pages to its description. She does though, correctly propose that the fight should be seen in the 'context of a growing revulsion against blood sports' as I have already outlined above[79]. It is not then, surprising that this fixed characterisation of the 'cruel' George Wombwell should rely so heavily on the events at Warwick. He would, for nearly two hundred years, be seen as both a cruel and a greedy man, stopping at little to make money from his animal charges.

From Hone's outcry at Bartholomew Fair where he castigates Wombwell for 'his brutal cupidity'at Warwick' in 1825 to Cowie's reliance on a limited newspaper investigation, George's character has thus far, been so efficiently evaluated and of course it makes for so much excitement and spectacle to believe the fights actually took place in the way the newspapers and journals recorded the brutal outcome[80].

Although it was not long before the whole affair was forgotten by the visitors to the menagerie as it travelled throughout the country, there was at least one occasion when locals took offence to Wombwell being in their town. *Bell's Life in London* carried a report of arson on the 22nd July 1827 thus:

> DIABOLICAL ACT – On Saturday last, Wombwell's Menagerie arrived in Dewsbury, on its way to Leeds Fair, and on Sunday morning, about 2 O'clock, some incendiary set fire to the large caravan, containing the elephant, by throwing upon it an ignited substance, wrapped in some cloth. Fortunately, an alarm was given by a person accidentally passing when the fire had only penetrated through the first covering of the caravan. The keepers were instantly roused, and by their prompt exertions, aided by those of a few of the inhabitants, the dreadful consequences were prevented which such a conflagration, if not suppressed in time, would have produced. It is horrible to think of the havoc and destruction which might have been effected by the stupendous powers of an enlarged elephant, and the ferocity of lions, tigers and other ferocious animals, all let loose in a state of great excitement. Strong suspicion attaches to some individuals in the town, but Mr. Wombwell, disliking the trouble and expense of a prosecution, declines taking any steps to bring the supposed offenders to justice[81].

But this 'violence' against the menagerie was an infrequently reported occurrence, and Wombwell's reputation, from his persistent travelling, seemed not to be greatly affected. As early as 1818, the menagerie was being referred to with phrases such as 'The greatest encomium' and 'we unhesitatingly pronounce' and suchlike, and one might have expected a downturn in his popularity through 1825 and beyond[82].

The arson attempt in Dewsbury may have been an isolated and unconnected case, but it is also possible that some of the people of Dewsbury took offence to the events at Warwick. By 1830, even the reports from Bartholomew Fair were glowing in their admiration for Wombwell's Menagerie. For instance,

> 'G. Wombwell […] is again presenting himself before the Citizens of London, and the frequenters of Bartholomew Fair, with confidence, asserts that notwithstanding the fame of his hitherto unrivalled Collection of Wild Beasts, Birds, and Reptiles, which have always given universal satisfaction'

was the report in an edition of the *Morning Advertiser*[83]. Even as early as September 1826, his menagerie was being praised for being 'the favourite resort of the visitors, however, seems to be Wombwell's menagerie, for there are young, the old, - even from the belle to the "unwashed artisan", evidently find amusement', stated one of the *Berkshire Chronicle's* articles[84].

There was however, another very concerning incident which

occurred during the 1826 Boughton Green Fair, in

Northamptonshire, according to the *Hereford Journal*[85].

It will be recollected that a very serious affray took place at Boughton Green Fair, Northamptonshire, last year, in consequence of an organised band of ruffians, who at the close of the fair commenced a general attack upon the booths, for the sake of plunder. Wombwell's Menagerie was twice attacked, and one of the assistants, who was particularly active in repelling the assailants, disappeared at the close of the conflict, and was supposed to have absconded with the receipts of the day. Nothing was heard of him till Saturday se'nnight, when preparations were making for the late fair. On clearing out the cellars which are generally used for the reception of ale, porter, &c. during the fair, under one of the thralls, a fur cap was found, and shortly afterwards the body of the poor fellow, who could only be known by his dress was discoved; his head appeared to have been dreadfully fractured, and there can be no doubt that he fell a martyr to his exertions, by some one of the assailants. The ruffians were headed by a pugilist of the name of George Catherall, who had assumed the name of Captain Slash, and was executed at Northampton.

Hereford Journal, Wednesday 11th July 1827

So even though Wombwell's reputation was not lastingly affected by the events at Warwick, and indeed he seemed to have benefitted financially from the extensive publicity, the very same events also became the myth on which the character of George Wombwell was foundered by some parts of the establishment and it is that viewpoint which appears to have been carried forward to today.

SPCA, Quakers, Printers and Newspaper conspiracy theories

Can we then, deduce any conspiracy against George Wombwell because of the lion fight at Warwick? There are several names that need exploring further, that were mentioned within the actual newspaper reports.

> Mr Wheeler, Inspector and Mr Martin M.P., from the SPCA
> S. Hoare, Quaker, and the letter-writer
> Mr Whitehead, Quaker, the alleged visitor to Warwick
> William Hone, printer and resident of the City of London

The first three, all being concerned with the notion of cruelty to animals, and at a time when Parliament was debating and passing an animal rights law, makes it possible they were in collusion at some point. However, I do not believe that to be the case. They appeared in the newspapers during both April and July because the papers had reproduced the alleged Warwick fight details on both occasions. The second occasion was a repeat of an earlier report and the first had turned out to be a complete hoax! Someone though, namely the original author of the fight report, knew names that would be associated with animal rights. We do not know who that author was, but in all likelihood could it have been Wombwell or another showman, as indicated by the fact that Mr James had reportedly set up a lion and dog fight during 1824 according to the report from *Bell's Life in London and Sporting Chronicle*, Sunday 10 April 1825.

> 'A bill was placed in our hands, issued by Earl James and Sons – the proprietors of the notorious *Bonassus* – in which we found an account, word for word, similar to that published yesterday, of a fight between same lion, and the same six dogs, alleged to have taken place for 600 sovereigns in Lancashire, on the 14th of January 1824.

It was the *Morning Herald* that had apparently first published this false report, but it was *Bell's Life in London* that had published it to support their own 'challenge' to George Wombwell. I believe what had happened was that the *Bell's* periodical had taken upon themselves to start the rumours off and that Mr Whitehead and Mr Hoare had got caught up in the frenzy around the numerous newspaper reports of the events at

Warwick. As for Mr Wheeler and Mr Martin, they were both making the newspapers due to the introduction of the first animal rights law and for committing guilty parties to large fines for cruel acts to domestic animals. *Bell's Life in London*, being a newspaper primarily for sports, would have known about the law and its consequences and if the report they had seen had been embellished with the names of Wheeler and Martin, it might have made it more authentic to the readers.

Bell's Life in London was primarily concerned with covering sporting events although it did start life as an anti-establishment paper covering general news and was aimed at working class readers. Its editor in 1824 was Vincent George Dowling (1785 – 1852), elder brother to Sir James Dowling (1787 – 1844), who, during his early life, became a skilled reporter on Parliamentary debate[86]. This would have been a useful skill, although Sir James, by 1824 had been called to the bar and was occupied on publishing *King's Bench Law Reports* between 1822 – 31.

Dowling was also an experienced reporter by the time he was made editor of the periodical. According to his Dictionary entry he also became prominent in making the boxing ring 'the means of making the manly love of fair play'. It is probably no coincidence that the first reports of the events at Warwick were published alongside reports of boxing matches like the one between Gem Ward and Tom Cannon. It is also unlikely to be a coincidence that the style of the Warwick reports followed the same reporting practices of boxing matches where journalistic language such as 'First Fight' and 'Second Fight' became popular in the columns of newspapers.

It is perfectly feasible that Vincent Dowling was at the heart of some conspiracy to defame Wombwell on the basis of cruelty to animals, and that he operated within a network that included establishment figures who had much to lose to an act of Parliament that might one day prevent many blood sports such as fox hunting, and even take control of the Royal sport of horse racing. The latter was something that *Bell's Life in London* was increasingly dependent on for their readership[87]. I do not believe the *Morning Herald* was a part of any conspiracy, Dowling having enough Parliamentary contacts to promote one all on his own. The *Herald's* editor during 1825 was another Irishman, Stanley Lees Gifford (1788 – 1858), so it is not beyond the bounds of possibility that it was discussed in the Coffee-Houses that populated the City of London at the time.

Why did George Wombwell get so much bad publicity?

I believe the reasons to be two-fold. Firstly, he was a victim of

his own entrepreneurship. By that I mean once a rumour had

been published, mostly during April 1825, George Wombwell,

seizing the opportunity, responded to the challenge after reading

the reports of a fictitious forthcoming fight, then destined to be

held at Worcester racecourse. His letter, dated 13th April and

published in *Bell's* periodical, rose to the challenge, except he

suggests Wallace as the lion he would put against the six dogs.

This seems to me to be the only letter published that possibly to

have come from George Wombwell.

Secondly, George Wombwell was an easy target that did not

upset any of the sporting fraternity, being a travelling showman.

He was well known across the whole country, so any bad

publicity about animal cruelty would be sure to spread

everywhere in the land. This would attract the attention of those

persons, as we have seen, that had progressive ideas on animal welfare and were in a position to do something about it. It would also detract attention from the sports, such as racing and fox hunting, where both horse and dog owners may have felt vulnerable to a new animal welfare law. Wombwell would have been a perfect distraction for those owners.

On the seedier side of racing and other sports, the gambling fraternity would have seen a fight between dogs and lions as an ideal vehicle for their betting habits. *Bell's Life in London* were always reporting on the latest announced contests and the betting that was whipped up by these gambling enthusiasts. Wombwell, allegedly wagering a fortune on his lions, would have gamblers flocking to the site of the fight to lay their own bets on the outcome, thus promoting the seedier side of the 'entertainment'.

William Hone, the other named protagonist

William Hone, the City-based printer, had produced a vitriolic

attack on Wombwell when the menagerie visited Bartholomew

Fair in 1825. He took offence to the advertising cloths which

displayed representations of the Warwick fight, so he had

claimed in his *Every-Day Book*. I believe that Hone's attack was

personal and not a part of some broader conspiracy. However,

one can never entirely count it out. He did though, republish in

his *Every-Day Book*, the newspaper account that mentions

Warwick as a 'hoax'. Therefore, I surmise that he must have

been outraged by some other factor than the account of the

Warwick fight. We do get a tantalizing hint of that in another

account from an amateur book printer, Charles Clark of Great

Totham Hall in Essex. One of Clark's letters, sent to his friend in

London, John Russell Smith, a London-based printer and

publisher, noted that when he met Wombwell at the Maldon

Fair:

> 'he [Wombwell] told me he had seen the
> scandalous article about him in Hone's *Every-*
> *Day Book* and told me how he offended Hone. He
> also gave me many hitherto unknown particulars
> respecting himself'[88].

This letter stops short of saying exactly how Wombwell had upset

Hone so much the latter set about a character assassination, but as

it was sent in 1838, 13 years had elapsed and Wombwell had still

remembered the event and the cause of it. I cannot believe that a

few adverse advertising cloths would stay in the mind of

Wombwell for that length of time, but I can believe that the

attempt to get Wombwell to become barred from Bartholomew

Fair, since Wombwell would have to go through the same

problems each year along with the other showmen, of getting his

booth accepted at each anniversary of the Fair. Hone's published

attack would appear each year at about the same time reminding

everyone of Hone' feelings towards Wombwell.

Clark must have read one of these later copies of the *Every-Day*

Book and had taken it upon himself to ask Wombwell about the affair once he had a chance to see him in person. Hone's comments must have also affected Clark, a fervent fan of Wombwell, and we shall return to Clark in Volume Two. Unfortunately, Clark does not elaborate further on Hone's reasons, but we can speculate that Hone would have had numerous contacts throughout the City, given his earlier libel trials as well as the 'friends' that had come to his rescue whilst in the debtor's prison. It might be that he was acting on behalf of one or more of them, to return a favour, particularly given the mounting tensions surrounding the existence of Bartholomew Fair within the City authorities.

Clark does though, provide a further clue in the same letter to Smith thus:

> 'He [Wombwell] told me too, that in all probability he should never 'stand' at Bartholomew Fair again, as the city authorities appeared to be inclined to raise still higher, their already exhorbitant charges for tolls.'

Here again, Wombwell's discussion with Clark of Bartholomew Fair, is evidence of its prominence in Wombwell's mind and of its particular importance to his annual income and prestige, but also that it would not happen 'at any price'.

Conclusions

Much like Caravaggio, a most misunderstood artist condemned in his own time for being heavily involved in late renaissance murder plots and other sword fighting exploits, George Wombwell becomes embroiled in the controversy of contemporary local politics surrounding the provision of public Fairs and, on a national basis, to an involvement with the earliest of the Animal Rights campaigns and Acts of Parliament for the prevention to cruelty to animals. He appears not to have done anything particular to warrant this attention other than being a travelling showman. Apart from capitalizing on the publicity surrounding the advertisements of the events at Warwick, seemingly made even more prominent after his alleged letters to newspaper editors, Wombwell may have become the innocent victim of the growing local opposition to Bartholomew Fair and to a national campaign for animal rights from members of the establishment committed to reforming animal welfare in Britain.

His high profile position across the country put him at risk of manipulation by newspaper editors, particularly *Bell's Life in London*, who appear to be at the heart of an underhand scheme to discredit Wombwell for violent acts that he had no intention of carrying out. Once the false reports of lion and dog fights had spread across the country via local and national newspapers, a false challenge had been offered to Wombwell through *Bell's Life in London*, with a cash reward and the offer of organising and overseeing the event, to include the sales of tickets for the event. This news was quickly picked up by animal rights reformers and religious factions alike. As the year progressed reports were written in such a manner to make it appear that Wombwell had ignored them all and was still insistent on carrying out the fight between a lion and six dogs at the Warwick racecourse.

Meanwhile, the gambling fraternity had started to offer odds through the newspapers, with a view to attract the betting fraternity to participate in the event by taking a gamble on the outcome. Reports of knuckle fights appeared alongside the lion fight and the style of these reports took on the format of the bare fist fight to add to the authenticity of the Warwick event. Even though *Bell's Life in London* eventually carried the report of the 'hoax', it continued to promote a mythical event, knowing that this would produce a diversion from the blood sports and horse racing, all of which might be subject to stricter restrictions or outright bans in some future animal rights legislation.

The late Georgian period was a turning point for animal welfare, as we have seen with beginnings of the SPCA. Even before its evolution there was a groundswell of opinion against animal cruelty. One such voice was William Hogarth (1697 –

Plate I: Hogarth's Four Stages of Cruelty, 1751

1764) who as early as 1751, produced a four print series entitled 'The Four Stages of Cruelty' that depicted the cruelty to animals that was happening around him in London at the time and the consequences of such violent actions. In the first and second plates, one Tom Nero, Hogarth's fictitious protagonist, is seen as both a child and an adult performing violent and cruel acts on animals. It the first plate he is seen attempting to insert an arrow into the anus of a dog, whilst others appear to be preventing Nero in his actions. Also in the picture is a dog fighting with a cat, kittens strung upside down from a post and a dog having its eyes

pierced out by a needle. These despicable acts, Hogarth is suggesting, represent the inhumanity of man he sees around him. In the second plate, Nero is seen in charge of a horse, clearly exhausted

Plate II: Hogarth's Four Stages of Cruelty, 1751

by fatigue, whilst four oversized men, probably representing lawyers, are being cast out the attached waggon, somewhat reluctantly. One might argue that even the full weight of the law could not save the horse from its destiny at the hands of Nero. The other two Hogarth plates represent what happens to Nero when he is convicted of murder and subsequently hanged, with his body being dissected and scrutinised within Surgeon's Hall in the City of London.

Although the scenes are fictitious we can see Hogarth's moral within the series. Put simply, those that deal out such cruelty as children will grow into violent and cruel adults and will suffer the consequences of their actions. Such representations, printed and made available for pennies, could be seen by most Londoners at the time.

There were never any reports up to 1825, that George Wombwell carried out similar crimes within his Menagerie. Nevertheless, he was chosen by the *Bell's* editor to represent him as a cruel person. This diversion from the reality of, for instance, the Smithfield meat industry, bull and bear baiting, horse racing and fox hunting, was convenient for some establishment figures. The original report, fictitious and written by an unknown showman, no doubt to boost audiences in earlier years, was repeated in the Summer

of 1825 to prolong the diversion as long as possible, in case

Parliament decided to consider amendments to include such

sporting activities.

Mr Martin, on the 24th March 1825, moved to bring in a Bill to

amend his Act for the protection against *Improper Treatment to*

Cattle[89]. The purpose was to increase the penalty from the fixed

two months' imprisonment, but proposed instead 'to leave the

punishment of it to the magistrates at quarter-sessions'. There was

opposition to the amendment and it was defeated on division. Mr

Martin summed up the proceedings as follows:

> 'Mr Martin said, he could not have believed, that any
> hon. member would have stood forward, as the hon.
> member for Reading had done, to defend the barbarities
> which were practised upon horses, and cattle. With re-
> gard to the anecdote which the hon. member had related
> respecting his adventures with the hackney-coachman, he
> would merely observe that, upon the hon. member's own
> showing, the hackney-coachman had taken the worst
> course in the world with his restive horses. The hon.
> member must be little of an equestrian, if he was not
> aware, that the most certain way to make a horse a starter
> was to beat it when it did start. He was sure the hon.
> member's constituents would not like the hon. member

the better, for the sentiments he had that night expressed. He said so, because he knew the hon. member would soon have a petition to present from them in favour of this bill. The hon. member, at the recurrence of another election, might find it difficult to secure his return ["order!"]. He was not out of order. He had one argument in support of his bill, which he thought would secure him the vote of the Attorney and Solicitor General. It was this. The present bill was a transcript of a bill which had been approved, some years ago, by all the law lords, by lord Ellenborough, lord Erskine, and last, though not least, by the present lord chancellor. He did not expect that mention of this last name would at all injure this bill with those gentlemen who were of opinion that "whatever is, is best." The present lord chancellor had approved of this bill, when it was sent down from the Lords to that House. He therefore trusted that the House would allow this bill to be introduced, notwithstanding the invidious sarcasms which had been thrown upon it.'

It is interesting to note that he mentions Lord Ellenborough (1790 – 1871) in his summing up. Ellenborough, as Chief Judge, had presided over the trial during 1817, of one James Watson and others for treason[90]. One of the key prosecution witnesses was Vincent George Dowling, later to become the editor of *Bell's Life in London*. Mr Dowling was called as he was one of the 'shorthand writers' that witnessed and recorded the speeches made to a mass meeting at Spa Fields in Islington, London on the 15th November and again on the 2nd December 1816.

Thought to be treasonable, the speech content was vital in secur-

ing a conviction. Dowling's evidence is recorded and published

in *Fairburn's Edition of the Whole Proceedings* (Fairburn, Lon-

don 1817)[91]. Although the content is not relevant to Womb-

well's history, it shows that Lord Ellenborough would have

known Dowling from this trial as well as from Dowling's fre-

quent visits to Parliament to cover proceedings. Martin's sug-

gestion that his Bill 'was a transcript of a bill which had been

approved, some years ago, by all the law lords, by Lord Ellen-

borough', is evidence enough to demonstrate the small world in

which these protagonists circulated.

Earlier that month Mr Martin had attempted to broaden the leg-

islation to account for the protection against blood sports such as

stag and fox hunting, that Martin referred to as 'barbarous

sport'. Again the motion was defeated on division. It must

though, have seemed inevitable that at some point in the future,

the Commons would introduce such legislation, so there was all the more reason to deflect attention away from the establish-ment's favourite sporting activities.

There are those that will say that the lion fight taking place is a better story, but it's just a story. 200 years of 'hamster moments' has taught us that. In the end, the paying public had all but forgotten the issue within a few months and Wombwell returned to his Bartholomew Fair booth time and time again to participate in the wonders of the natural world, which he supplied in abundance. He went on to have three Menageries, simultaneously travelling the countryside of Britain and elsewhere. In the next part we shall see how George Wombwell, from a position of being close to fashionable London society, became the nation's favourite travelling Menagerist and how he coped with fame, fortune and failures before his death in November 1850.

End Notes and Bibliography

[1] Kurt Koenigsberger, *The Novel and the Menagerie, Totality, Englishness and Empire,* (Ohio State University, Columbus 2007) p. 23

[2] Helen Langdon, *Caravaggio A Life* (Pimlico, London 1999) pp. 267 - 68

[3] Note that where newspaper articles have been reproduced in type form, the original spelling and grammar have been retained, except where spelling is likely to cause a distraction.

[4] Sir Leslie Stephen, Dictionary of National Biography, Volume 62 (Macmillan, New York 1885) p. 345 - 6

[5] *Jackson's Oxford Journal (Oxford, England),* Saturday, July 2, 1825; Issue 3766

[6] *Jackson's Oxford Journal (Oxford, England),* Saturday, July 23, 1825;

[7] *The Examiner (London, England),* Sunday, July 24, 1825; Issue 912

[8] *The Examiner (London, England),* Sunday, July 24, 1825; Issue 912

[9] *Caledonian Mercury (Edinburgh, Scotland),* Monday, July 25, 1825; Issue 16213

[10] *Hampshire Telegraph and Sussex Chronicle etc. (Portsmouth, England),* Monday, July 25, 1825; Issue 1346

[11] *The Morning Chronicle (London, England),* Thursday, July 28, 1825; Issue 1753

[12] *Jackson's Oxford Journal (Oxford, England),* Saturday, July 30, 1825; Issue 3770

[13] *The Examiner (London, England),* Sunday, July 31, 1825; Issue 913

[14] *The Times (London),* Thursday August 4, 1825; Issue 12723

[15] *Caledonian Mercury (Edinburgh, Scotland),* Saturday, August 20, 1825; Issue 16224

[16] *Caledonian Mercury (Edinburgh, Scotland),* Saturday, September 10, 1825; Issue 16233

[17] *The Morning Chronicle (London, England),* Tuesday, September 6, 1825; Issue 17567

[18] *Berrow's Worcester Journal (Worcester, England),* Thursday, September 08, 1825; Issue 6401

[19] *The Morning Chronicle (London, England),* Saturday, July 30, 1825; Issue 17535

[20] *The Morning Chronicle (London, England),* Thursday, July 28, 1825; Issue 17533

[21] *The Morning Chronicle (London, England),* Tuesday, August 2, 1825; Issue 17537

[22] *The Morning Post (London, England),* Wednesday, August 10, 1825; Issue 17048

[23] *The Morning Post (London, England),* Monday, August 15, 1825; Issue

17052

[24] *The Bury and Norwich Post, (Bury Saint Edmunds, England)*, Wednesday, November 09, 1825

[25] This must be one of the 'two housekeepers' in the previous reports.

[26] William Hone, *The Every-Day Book, or, The Guide to the Year; relating the Popular Amusements, Sports, Ceremonies, Manners, Customs and Events incident to the 365 days in Present and past Times, being a series of 5000 Anecdotes and facts, forming the history of the year, the calendar of the seasons, and a Chronological Dictionary of the Almanac, with a Variety of Important and Diverting Information, for Daily Use and Entertainment, compiled from Authentic Sources* (Hone, London, 1825)

[27] Hone, p. 493

[28] Hone p. 495

[29] Hone, pp. 1197 – 99 also at http://honearchive.org/etexts/edb/day-pages/248-sep05.html [Accessed 15th September 2015]

[30] The Sun from March 13, 1986

[31] Hone, p 1252

[32] Declared bankrupt 16th October 1810 and during April 1825

[33] William Hone, George Cruikshank, *The Political Showman at Home – Exhibiting his cabinet of curiosities and creatures – all alive* (Hone, London 1821), probably from a much earlier incarnation: Bandogge, not being a breed but a function, in this case for guarding and protecting purposes.

[34] George Cruikshank, 'A Peep at Bartholomew Fair', *George Cruikshank's Omnibus* (Tilt & Bogue, London 1842) p. 188 – 191 http://www.gutenberg.org/files/47400/47400-h/47400-h.htm#A_PEEP_AT_BARTHOLOMEW_FAIR [Accessed 15th September 2015]

[35] http://web.archive.org/web/20090327103512/http://www.cityoflondon.gov.uk/nr/rdonlyres/24b6c04d-ff99-445d-a2ca-7e618b42bf85/0/lh_gag_b3smithfieldmarketinformation.pdf [Accessed 10th May 2016]

[36] Richard Martin became known as 'Humanity Dick'.

[37] *The Morning Post*, February 12th, 1824

[38] Richard Martin, *Bear Baiting*, Hansard, HC 11th February 1824 vol 10 cc131-4

[39] https://www.animallaw.info/article/history-rspca [Accessed 28th September 2015]

[40] No Author, 'Smithfield Cattle Market', *The Farmer's Magazine*, Volume 19, January – June, 1849, p. 142

[41] No Author, 'Petition of the Merchant Bankers of London', *The Farmer's Magazine*, Volume 19, January – June, 1849, p. 144

[42] Hone, p799

[43] John Strutt, *The Sports and Pastimes of the People of England* (Hone, London 1826) p. xxxiv

[44] *The Blackburn Standard (Blackburn, England)*, Wednesday, December 26, 1849; Issue 780

[45] Eliza Cook, *Eliza Cook's Journal*, Volumes 1-2, October 1849, (John Owen, London 1849) p. 339

[46] *The Bury and Norwich Post (Bury Saint Edmunds, England)*, Wednesday, September 07, 1825; Issue 2254

[47] *The Standard (London, England)*, Friday, July 11, 1828; Issue 359

[48] *The Sheffield Independent, and Yorkshire and Derbyshire Advertiser (Sheffield, England)*, Saturday, May 28, 1831; Issue 597

[49] *The Leicester Chronicle: or, Commercial and Agricultural Advertiser* (Leicester, England), Saturday, August 05, 1837; pg. [1]; Issue 1394.

[50] Cruelty to Animals Act 1835

[51] Mr Marmaduke Lawson (Boroughbridge), Commons sitting, February 1st 1819, Hansard
http://hansard.millbanksystems.com/commons/1819/feb/01/wild-animals-reclaimed#S1V0039P0_18190201_HOC_162 [Accessed 26th January 2016]

[52] The *Liverpool Mercury (Liverpool, England)*, Friday, July 29, 1825

[53] *Hampshire Telegraph and Sussex Chronicle (Portsmouth, England)*, Monday, April 11, 1825; Issue 1331

[54] *The Morning Chronicle (London, England)*, Monday, April 4, 1825; Issue 17461

[55] Exeter 'Change was a menagerie of many years standing, popular with Royalty and the aristocracy. It was on the site on which the Strand Palace Hotel stands today.

[56] Helen Cowie, *Exhibiting Animals in Nineteenth-Century Britain: Empathy, Education, Entertainment* (Palgrave, Basingstoke 2014) p. 70

[57] *The Morning Post*, Friday 18th May 1821

[58] *The Morning Chronicle*, Wednesday 13th June 1821

[59] Helen Cowie, p. 70 – 1

[60] http://georgewombwell.omeka.net/items/show/5 [Accessed January 19th 2016]

[61] *Bell's Life in London and Sporting Chronicle (London, England)*, Sunday, July 17, 1825; pg. 229; Issue 177

[62] *Caledonian Mercury (Edinburgh, Scotland)*, Thursday, February 24, 1825; Issue 16148

[63] Ward (1800 -1884) was a bare knuckle fighter sometimes throughout his career referred to as The Black Diamond. This match took place on 19 July 1825 at Warwick on a very hot day with the temperature reputedly over 90 degrees Fahrenheit

[64] *The Times (London)*, Monday June 6th 1825; Issue 12672

[65] *Hampshire Telegraph and Sussex Chronicle etc. (Portsmouth, England)*, Monday, April 11, 1825; Issue 1331

[66] *Berrow's Worcester Journal (Worcester, England)*, Thursday, April 07, 1825; Issue 6379

[67] *Berrow's Worcester Journal (Worcester, England)*, Thursday, April 07, 1825; Issue 6379

[68] *Berrow's Worcester Journal (Worcester, England)*, Thursday, May 19, 1825; Issue 6385

[69] Bell's Life in London and Sporting Chronicle (London, England), 6th March 1825

[70] Joseph Jacobs, *Aesop's Fables* (Hayes Barton Press, North Carolina 2005) p. 9

[71] *Bell's Life in London and Sporting Chronicle,* Sunday 03 April 1825

[72] *Bell's Life in London and Sporting Chronicle*, Sunday 10 April 1825

[73] *Bells Life in London and Sporting Chronicle*, Sunday 15 May 1825

[74] *Bell's Life in London and Sporting Chronicle*, Sunday 31 July 1825

[75] *Bells Life in London and Sporting Chronicle*, Sunday 07 August 1825

[76] listen to the other side – It is the principle that no person should be judged without a fair hearing in which each party is given the opportunity to respond to the evidence against them

[77] *Berkshire Chronicle,* Saturday 09 April 1825

[78] *Worcester Journal*, Thursday, April 7th; Issue 6379

[79] Cowie, eBook location 2740 [Accessed April 8th 2016]

[80] See Hone's Daybook entry above

[81] *Bells Life in London and Sporting Chronicle*, Sunday 22 July 1827

[82] *Cheltenham Chronicle*, Thursday 06 August 1818

[83] *Morning Advertiser*, Friday, 03 September 1830

[84] *Berkshire Chronicle*, Saturday 23rd September 1826

[85] *Hereford Journal*, Wednesday 11th July 1827

[86] Sir Leslie Stephen, Dictionary of National Biography, Volume 15 (Macmillan, New York 1885) p. 390 - 1

[87] In 1831 *Bell's Life in London* was given over entirely to racing and was bought out by *The Sporting Life* in 1886.

[88] Charles Clark, *Letter 27th October 1838*, Essex Records Office, D/DU 668/1-4

[89] Mr Richard Martin, *Ill Treatment of Animals Bill*, Hansard, HC Deb 24 March 1825 vol 12 cc1160-2 http://hansard.millbanksystems.com/commons/1825/mar/24/ill-treatment-of-animals-bill [Accessed 26th January 2016]

[90] John Fairburn, *The Whole Proceedings on the Trial of John Watson for High Treason* (Fairburn, London 1817)

[91] John Fairburn, various pages of the transcript.

Bibliography

Bell's Life in London and Sporting Chronicle, 6th March 1825

Bell's Life in London and Sporting Chronicle, Sunday 10 April 1825

Bells Life in London and Sporting Chronicle, Sunday 17 April 1825

Bells Life in London and Sporting Chronicle, Sunday 15 May 1825

Bell's Life in London and Sporting Chronicle, Sunday, July 17, 1825; pg. 229; Issue 177

Bell's Life in London and Sporting Chronicle, Sunday 31 July 1825

Bells Life in London and Sporting Chronicle, Sunday 07 August 1825

Bells Life in London and Sporting Chronicle, Sunday 22 July 1827

Berkshire Chronicle, Saturday 09 April 1825

Berkshire Chronicle, Saturday 23rd September 1826

Berrow's Worcester Journal (Worcester, England), Thursday, September 08, 1825; Issue 6401

Berrow's Worcester Journal (Worcester, England), Thursday, April 07, 1825; Issue 6379

Berrow's Worcester Journal (Worcester, England), Thursday, May 19, 1825; Issue 6385

The Blackburn Standard (Blackburn, England), Wednesday, December 26, 1849; Issue 780

The Bury and Norwich Post (Bury Saint Edmunds, England), Wednesday, September 07, 1825; Issue 2254

The Bury and Norwich Post, (Bury Saint Edmunds, England), Wednesday, November 09, 1825

Caledonian Mercury (Edinburgh, Scotland), Thursday, February 24, 1825; Issue 16148

Caledonian Mercury (Edinburgh, Scotland), Monday, July 25, 1825; Issue 16213

Caledonian Mercury (Edinburgh, Scotland), Saturday, August 20, 1825; Issue 16224

Caledonian Mercury (Edinburgh, Scotland), Saturday, September 10, 1825; Issue 16233

Cheltenham Chronicle, Thursday 06 August 1818

Clark, Charles, *Letter 27th October 1838,* Essex Records Office, D/DU 668/1-4

Cruikshank, George 'A Peep at Bartholomew Fair' in George *Omnibus (Tilt & Bogue, London 1842) p. 188 – 191 also at* *http://www.gutenberg.org/files/47400/47400-h/47400-h.htm#A_PEEP_AT_BARTHOLOMEW_FAIR*

Cowie, Helen, *Exhibiting Animals in Nineteenth-Century Britain: Empathy, Education, Entertainment* (Palgrave, Basingstoke 2014)

The Examiner (London, England), Sunday, July 24, 1825; Issue 912

The Examiner (London, England) Sunday, July 31, 1825; Issue 913

Fairburn, John, *The Whole Proceedings on the Trial of John Watson for High Treason* (Fairburn, London 1817)

Hampshire Telegraph and Sussex Chronicle etc (Portsmouth, England), Monday, April 11, 1825; Issue 1331

Hampshire Telegraph and Sussex Chronicle etc. (Portsmouth, England) Monday, July 25, 1825; Issue 1346

Hereford Journal, Wednesday 11th July 1827

Hone, William, *The Every-Day Book*, (Hone, London, 1825) also at *http://honearchive.org/etexts/edb/day-pages/248-sep05.html*

Jackson's Oxford Journal (Oxford, England), Saturday, July 2, 1825; Issue 3766

Jackson's Oxford Journal (Oxford, England), Saturday, July 30, 1825; Issue 3770

Jacobs, Joseph, *Aesop's Fables* (Hayes Barton Press, North Carolina 2005)

Koenigsberger, Kurt, *The Novel and the Menagerie, Totality, Englishness and Empire,* (Ohio State University, Columbus 2007)

Langdon, Helen, 'Caravaggio A Life' (Pimlico, London 1999)

Liverpool Mercury etc. (Liverpool, England), Friday, July 29, 1825

The Leicester Chronicle: or, Commercial and Agricultural Advertiser (Leicester, England), Saturday, August 05, 1837; p. 1, Issue 1394

Lawson, Marmaduke, *Wild Animals Reclaimed,* House of

Commons sitting, February 1st 1819, Hansard, vol 39 cc200-2

Martin, Richard, *Bear Baiting*, House of Commons Sitting, 11th February 1824, Hansard vol 10 cc131-4

Martin, Richard, *Ill Treatment of Animals Bill*, House of Commons Sitting, 24th March, 1825, Hansard, vol 12 cc1160-2

Morning Advertiser, Friday, 03 September 1830

The Morning Chronicle, (London, England), Wednesday 13th June 1821

The Morning Chronicle (London, England), Monday, April 4, 1825; Issue 17461

The Morning Chronicle (London, England), Thursday, July 28, 1825; Issue 17533

The Morning Chronicle (London, England), Saturday, July 30, 1825; Issue 17535

The Morning Chronicle (London, England), Tuesday, August 2, 1825; Issue 17537

The Morning Chronicle (London, England), Tuesday, September 6, 1825; Issue 17567

The Morning Post, Friday 18th May 1821

The Morning Post, (London, England), February 12th 1824

The Morning Post (London, England), 5th August 1825

The Morning Post (London, England), Wednesday, August 10, 1825; Issue 17048

The Morning Post (London, England), Monday, August 15, 1825; Issue 17052

No Author, 'Smithfield Cattle Market', *The Farmer's Magazine*, , Volume 19, January – June, 1849

No Author, 'Petition of the Merchant Bankers of London', *The Farmer's Magazine*, Volume 19, January – June, 1849

The Sheffield Independent, and Yorkshire and Derbyshire Advertiser (Sheffield, England), Saturday, May 28, 1831; Issue 597

The Standard (London, England), Friday, July 11, 1828; Issue 359

Stephen, Sir Leslie (Ed.), *Dictionary of National Biography*, Volumes 15, 62 (Macmillan, New York 1885)

Strutt, Joseph, Hone, William, *The Sports and Pastimes of the People of England* (Thomas Tegg, London 1838)

The Times(London), Monday June 6th 1825; Issue 12672

The Times(London), Thursday August 4, 1825; Issue 12723

Worcester Journal, Thursday, April 7th; Issue 6379

Made in the USA
Charleston, SC
02 July 2016